PSYCHOLOGY PRACTITIONER GUIDEBOOKS

EDITORS
Arnold P. Goldstein, Syracuse University
Leonard Krasner, Stanford University & SUNY at Stony Brook
Sol L. Garfield, Washington University in St. Louis

TREATING CONDUCT AND OPPOSITIONAL DEFIANT DISORDERS IN CHILDREN

Pergamon Titles of Related Interest

Dangel/Polster TEACHING CHILD MANAGEMENT SKILLS
Feindler/Ecton ADOLESCENT ANGER CONTROL:
Cognitive-Behavioral Techniques
Goldstein/Glick/Irwin/Pask-McCartney/Rubama REDUCING
DELINQUENCY: Intervention in the Community
Hollin COGNITIVE-BEHAVIORAL INTERVENTIONS WITH YOUNG
OFFENDERS
White THE TROUBLED ADOLESCENT

Related Journals
(Free sample copies available upon request)

CHILD ABUSE AND NEGLECT
CHILDREN AND YOUTH SERVICES REVIEW
CLINICAL PSYCHOLOGY REVIEW
JOURNAL OF CHILD PSYCHOLOGY AND PSYCHIATRY
AND ALLIED DISCIPLINES
JOURNAL OF SCHOOL PSYCHOLOGY

TREATING CONDUCT AND OPPOSITIONAL DEFIANT DISORDERS IN CHILDREN

ARTHUR M. HORNE
University of Georgia

THOMAS V. SAYGER
University of Wisconsin, Madison

PERGAMON PRESS
Member of Maxwell Macmillan Pergamon Publishing Corporation
New York • Oxford • Beijing • Frankfurt
São Paulo • Sydney • Tokyo • Toronto

LP

Pergamon Press Offices:

U.S.A.   Pergamon Press, Inc., Maxwell House, Fairview Park,
                     Elmsford, New York 10523, U.S.A.

U.K.   Pergamon Press plc, Headington Hill Hall,
                     Oxford OX3 0BW, England

PEOPLE'S REPUBLIC Pergamon Press, 0909 China World Tower
OF CHINA   No. 1 Jian Guo Men Wai Avenue, Beijing 100004, China

FEDERAL REPUBLIC   Pergamon Press GmbH, Hammerweg 6,
OF GERMANY   D-6242 Kronberg, Federal Republic of Germany

BRAZIL   Pergamon Editora Ltda, Rua Eça de Queiros, 346,
                     CEP 04011, Paraiso, São Paulo, Brazil

AUSTRALIA   Pergamon Press Australia Pty Ltd., P.O. Box 544,
                     Potts Point, NSW 2011, Australia

JAPAN   Pergamon Press, 8th Floor, Matsuoka Central Building,
                     1-7-1 Nishishinjuku, Shinjuku-ku, Tokyo 160, Japan

CANADA   Pergamon Press Canada Ltd., Suite 271, 253 College Street,
                     Toronto, Ontario M5T 1R5, Canada

Copyright © 1990 Pergamon Press, Inc.

Library of Congress Cataloging in Publication Data

Horne, Arthur M., 1942-
    Treating conduct and oppositional defiant disorders in children /
Arthur M. Horne, Thomas V. Sayger.
    p. cm. -- (Psychology practitioner guidebooks)
    ISBN 0-08-036438-1 :   -- ISBN 0-08-036437-3 (soft) :
    1. Conduct disorders in children--Treatment. 2. Oppositional
defiant disorders in children--Treatment. 3. Family psychotherapy.
I. Sayger, Thomas V. II. Title. III. Series.
    [DNLM: 1. Antisocial Personality Disorder--in infancy & childhood.
2. Antisocial Personality Disorder--therapy. 3. Child Behavior
Disorders--therapy. 4. Family Therapy. 5. Social Environment. WS
350.6 H815t]
RJ506.C65H67   1990
618.92'89--dc20
DNLM/DLC
for Library of Congress   89-72168
                                                                 CIP

Printing: 1 2 3 4 5 6 7 8 9 Year: 0 1 2 3 4 5 6 7 8 9

Printed in the United States of America

⊚™

The paper used in this publication meets the minimum requirements of
American National Standard for Information Sciences -- Permanence of
Paper for Printed Library Materials, ANSI Z39.48-1984

10/09/90

Dedication

This book is dedicated to our families with appreciation for all they have given to us, and to Gerald R. Patterson, who provided the foundation for our understanding and treatment of behavior-disordered children and their families.

Contents

Acknowledgments

The various research projects conducted through the Family Therapy Research Project at Indiana State University provided much of the material presented in this book. Several of the projects were generously funded by the Indiana State University Research Committee. Appreciation is expressed to this committee and to Dean Mary Ann Carroll for her support and encouragement.

A number of faculty and students have been involved with the Family Therapy Research Project over the last decade, and their support and contributions are gratefully acknowledged. Appreciation is particularly expressed for the participation of faculty members Drs. Michele Boyer, Reece Chaney, John Jessell, and Laurence Passmore, and to program graduates Lisa Colpe, Jim Davison, Joan Fuelle Engstrom, Brian Glaser, Linda Haubold, Cliff Heegel, Leslie James, Paul Morris, Alan Reid, Mary Van Valkenburg, Barry Van Dyck, John Walker, and Alice Whalen, whose doctoral research was conducted through the Family Therapy Research Project. Special thanks go to Elaine Landes for her contributions to our understanding and use of the word processing of this text. Appreciation is also expressed to Brian Glaser, Joan Fuelle Engstrom, and Rebecca A. Dyer for their critical reading of early drafts of the manuscript, Dr. Thomas Achenbach for information regarding assessment instruments, and Peter Manesis for assistance with graphics.

Preface

Conduct and oppositional defiant disorders in children represent a predominant childhood referral problem, accounting for the majority of presenting problems to child and family agencies. Aggressive and disruptive behavior is one of the more enduring dysfunctions of children and, if left untreated, frequently results in high personal and emotional — as well as financial — costs to the child, the family, and society in general.

This book represents a decade of clinical treatment for and research with conduct-disordered children using a family intervention model in research centers and community agencies. The individuals employing this model, both clinicians and researchers, have the vision of developing a program that provides effective remediation of childhood behavioral problems, establishment of happy, healthy, and functional family units, and an ongoing link between clinical practice and research.

The comprehensive treatment of childhood behavior disorders requires the integration of many theoretical ideals into one flexible, yet pragmatically sound, treatment approach. The treatment of choice for behavior disorders in children is behavioral family therapy which links a number of treatment modes for dysfunctional children and their families. This approach combines the basic principles of behavior change — including the reinforcement of prosocial behaviors and the extinguishing or punishing of aversive actions of behavioral psychology — with the methods of cognitive behavioral therapy for assisting individuals and family members to understand the relationship between thoughts, behaviors, and affective responses. Additionally, the theoretical and practical bases for understanding and encouraging change in behavior, cognitions, and environmental influences of social learning theory are combined with the family systems therapy framework for understanding the development and management of dysfunctional family systems. We have found these theories to be compatible, and also useful in conceptualizing treatment needs for families dealing with child behavior problems.

Chapters 1 and 2 in this book present an overview of the nature of the problem of conduct- and oppositional-defiant-disordered children and explanations for the development of dysfunctional behaviors in children. Chapter 3 offers a brief synopsis of treatment programs which have been utilized with disruptive behavior-disordered children and their family members, while Chapter 4 presents assessment procedures and instruments to help the clinician obtain diagnostic information and initiate treatment in a family context. Chapters 5 through 9 discuss the crux of the treatment plan including the initial stages of treatment, establishing positive expectations for change and a success orientation, implementing change strategies for both overt and cognitive behaviors and environmental situations, monitoring client progress, and creating effective family interaction patterns. Chapter 10 presents strategies for maintenance and identifies issues for extending and generalizing the program beyond the immediate family to include social service agencies, schools, and extended family members. The remaining chapter emphasizes the importance of evaluating treatment success and considerations for additional applications of the treatment strategies.

While working with families, we attempt to develop a positive expectation for change because family members need to experience the feeling of being understood and positively valued. The family has undoubtedly been told by a variety of professionals (e.g., teachers, caseworkers, psychologists, counselors) what they have done wrong; therefore, our approach is to determine what the family has been doing right and to encourage further development of more effective behaviors. The family members must feel secure in making changes if maintenance is to be ensured. The program format in this book is presented in logical and sequential steps, although there is considerable flexibility in the ways the intervention is presented to families. Our approach is an evolving process and we hope the material presented will be useful, while at the same time acknowledging the growing, open, and flexible nature of this treatment model.

Chapter 1
Introduction and Overview

DEFINING OPPOSITIONAL DEFIANT AND CONDUCT DISORDERS

Psychologists, psychiatrists, counselors, social workers, and child development experts have devoted considerable time and effort to defining behavior disorders. Definitions are available in the *Diagnostic and Statistical Manual of Mental Disorders* (DSM-III-R) (American Psychiatric Association [APA], 1987) that provide clear delineations and guidelines for determining both the existence of a particular condition and the extent to which it manifests itself.

The DSM-III-R defines oppositional defiant disorder as

a pattern of negativistic, hostile, and defiant behavior without the more serious violations of the basic rights of others that are seen in Conduct Disorder. . . . Children with this disorder commonly are argumentative with adults, frequently lose their temper, swear, and are often angry, resentful, and easily annoyed by others. They frequently actively defy adult requests or rules and deliberately annoy other people. They tend to blame others for their own mistakes or difficulties. (p.56)

Oppositional defiant disorders typically are evident in the home, but they may or may not be present outside the home, at school, with friends, or in a clinical interview. The following diagnostic criteria have been presented in the DSM-III-R:

A disturbance of at least six months during which at least five of the following are present:

1. Often loses temper
2. Often argues with adults
3. Often actively defies or refuses adult requests or rules
4. Often deliberately does things that annoy other people
5. Often blames others for his or her own mistakes
6. Is often touchy or easily annoyed by others

7. Is often angry and resentful
8. Is often spiteful or vindictive
9. Often swears or uses obscene language. (pp. 57–58)

A more disruptive form of behavioral problem is the conduct disorder. Conduct disorders are of three types: group, solitary aggressive, and undifferentiated. As the names imply, group conduct disorders are most commonly evident when the person is with peers, whereas the solitary aggressive type usually manifests itself as aggressive physical behavior toward adults or peers but not as a function of group or gang activity. The undifferentiated type represents a mixture of clinical characteristics. The DSM-III-R defines conduct disorder as

> a persistent pattern of conduct in which the basic rights of others and major age-appropriate societal norms or rules are violated. The behavior pattern typically is present in the home, at school, with peers, and in the community. The conduct problems are more serious than those seen in Oppositional Defiant Disorder. . . . Physical aggression is common. Children or adolescents with this disorder usually initiate aggression, may be physically cruel to other people or to animals, and frequently deliberately destroy other people's property. . . . They may engage in stealing with confrontation of the victim, as in mugging, extortion, or armed robbery. At later ages, the physical violence may take the form of rape, assault, or, in rare cases, homicide. (p.53)

Often conduct disorder problems are preceded by other problems, including oppositional defiant disorder, attention deficit disorder, and family dysfunction. The diagnostic criteria for conduct disorder (APA, 1987) are:

> A distrubance of conduct lasting at least six months in which at least three of the following have been present:
>
> 1. Has stolen without confrontation of a victim on more than one occasion
> 2. Has run away from home overnight at least twice while living in parental or surrogate home
> 3. Often lies
> 4. Has deliberately engaged in fire setting
> 5. Is often truant from school
> 6. Has broken into someone else's house, building, or car
> 7. Has deliberately destroyed others' property
> 8. Has been physically cruel to animals
> 9. Has forced someone to have sexual activity with him or her
> 10. Has used a weapon in more than one fight
> 11. Often initiates physical fights
> 12. Has stolen with confrontation of a victim
> 13. Has been physically cruel to people. (p. 55)

Researchers have devoted books to the presentation of coding systems for determining whether and to what degree specific behavioral disorders are present in children (Reid, 1978) and the development of empirically based assessment processes in order to identify problems of children (Achenbach & McConaughy, 1987).

While researchers and third-party payment services attend closely to precise definitions, parents, teachers, and managers of public establishments (such as fast-food restaurants and discount department stores) are less precise but often no less accurate in their ability to identify behavioral disorders. Parents are often able to explain that their children have behavioral problems. One stated:

> He was born bad. From the day he came home he was trouble. Cried. Got in trouble as soon as he could. He couldn't keep his hands off nothing. . . he was everywhere. I knew he'd be trouble when he got to school, and I was right. He'll pick a disagreement with anybody. But he sure can be lovable.

Not all parents are able to clearly define their children as having behavioral problems because many do not define fighting, disobeying, or poor school habits as problems; rather these are seen as normal conditions of children from their familial or socioeconomic background. The teachers of their children, however, are usually quite capable of identifying the disruptive behavior. Teachers have a large sample of students to observe annually and, from this group, recognize the range of problem behaviors. It is often behavioral problem children who receive special attention from teachers. Teachers are also the people most likely to point out to parents that their children demonstrate behavioral disorders and suggest referrals to professional services.

The authors have conducted a family research project since 1980. The majority of referrals to the program come from teachers, school counselors or psychologists, and principals. Other referrals are from courts, child protective services, churches, and related areas. When we work with a school and ask teachers to identify children with behavioral disorders, there is little hesitation. Usually, they are able to point out two or three students per class who demonstrate more disruptive behavior than the average. Teachers are provided with a brief description of the behaviors we are looking for:

> We are seeking "aggressive" children who have demonstrated difficulties in adjusting to school, their teachers, or their peers. These children exhibit their difficulties by engaging in selected behaviors, e.g., "hit, kicked, or shoved a child." We are seeking children who, in your judgment, would require additional attention for disruptive/aggressive behavior if such services were available. Following is a list of some of the behavioral descriptors for "disruptive:"

Out of seat often	Speaks out of turn
Disruptive noises	Interrupts
Does not listen	Giggles in silly way
Rummages shelves/cupboard	Cries over small matters
Hits, kicks, shoves	Argues in angry way
Takes something from another child	Repeatedly asks same question
	Makes fun of another
Defies teacher	Forces someone to do something
Throws an object at someone	they don't want to do
Refuses to share	Destroys property
Curses	

From this description teachers are able to quite accurately identify children with oppositional defiant, conduct, and attention deficit disorders, although they frequently do not discriminate among these disorders. Rather, they use the more encompassing expressions "acting out" or "disruptive."

There is good justification for using broader terms for behavioral problems of children, for whereas the DSM-III-R presents the categories distinctly, in practice there is considerable overlap. Werry, Reeves, and Elkind (1987) have reported that the coexistence of attention deficit and conduct disorders is probably common. Coexistence of these disorders increases the degree of disability, and it is these children who are more likely to be referred for treatment. Thus, Werry et al. (1987) argue that the dispute as to whether the child's diagnosis should be attention deficit or conduct disorder is not very important because most cases seen in clinics will have both disorders as defining characteristics.

Werry et al. (1987) concluded there may well be some distinct differences among the disorders, with attention deficit being more a male disorder, overwhelmingly more so than conduct or oppositional defiant disorder. Further, attention deficit has an earlier onset, although conduct disorders may be presented at clinics as early as other deviant behavior disorders. Attention deficit appears primarily to be a disorder of cognitive impairment, more a function of impulsive responding and poorer achievement in school, and is possibly associated with increased motor activity and neurodevelopment abnormalities. The common association of attention deficit and conduct disorders seems to retain the negative features of each disorder and increases the degree of the handicap.

Reeves, Werry, Elkind, and Zametkin (1987) stated that conduct disorder seems to be a disorder with an early onset marked by egocentricity, aggressiveness, poor interpersonal relationships, and an adverse child-rearing environment. They suggested that oppositional defiant disorder and conduct disorder may well be the same condition, except that oppositional defiant disorder may be more common in girls, which suggests that it may be a less severe form of conduct disorder. In a study assessing the diagnoses of 108 children using DSM-III-R criteria, Reeves et al. (1987) found only four children with a conduct disorder diagnosis unaccompanied by any other diagnosis, and only two children had an oppositional defiant disorder diagnosis alone. In a comparison of clinically diagnosed children and a control group of normal children, Reeves et al. (1987) found that children with attention deficit disorder and conduct disorder had a much higher frequency of adverse family backgrounds and were characterized by fathers with lower education levels, family alcoholism, and fathers with antisocial personalities. These children did not differ significantly from the normal group in terms of marital adjustment of parents or parental strife observed by the child. It may be that there is an interaction between the cognitive impairment condition of attention deficit disorder and psychosocial environmental factors that contribute to conduct and oppositional defiant disorders. This interaction may result in clinical cases warranting attention because of the difficulties caused in classrooms, the conflict in families, and the personal pain that children with this condition experience.

Kazdin, Esveldt-Dawson, French, and Unis (1987) used the term "antisocial behaviors" to describe children who commit aggressive acts, steal, lie, and engage in other activities that are major social rule violations. They reported that the clinical significance of the antisocial behaviors is reflected in their relatively high prevalence and clinical referral rates, their stability and poor prognosis over the course of development, and their continuity within families across multiple generations. Further, antisocial children show serious dysfunction in their interactions in and out of the home. Their behavior is also associated with a variety of maladaptive cognitive processes (e.g., deficits in problem-solving skills, attributing hostile intent to others). This finding is consistent with the work of Reeves et al. (1987), which indicated that deficits in cognitive skills may be expected when aggressive behavior in children is encountered.

The work the present authors have done with their Family Therapy Research Project has yielded results consistent with those of Kazdin et al. (1987), Reeves et al. (1987), and Werry et al. (1987). After teachers have identified and referred aggressive or disorderly students and the parents confirm, through self-report, that the child is aggressive, the Child Behavior Checklist (CBCL) (Achenbach & Edelbrock, 1983) is used as one source of confirming conduct or oppositional defiant disorders. We have found that of 151 children referred for treatment with T scores at or above 65 (scores at or above the 93rd percentile) on the aggressive subscale (group mean = 75), the mean score on the hyperactivity sub-scale for the group was 72, placing the average aggressive child above the 98th percentile on hyperactivity. This finding indicates that students with a high aggression score are likely to be impulsive and to demonstrate ineffective problem-solving skills and poor classroom attending skills. This has been confirmed by classroom observations of children referred for treatment in our program. In a study of 102 nonaggressive control students, we found mean scores of 56 on the aggressive and hyperactive subscales, indicating scores in the normal range for both areas. Other subscale scores are reflective of the aggressive pattern shown by students referred for treatment, as indicated in Table 1.1.

This diagnostic profile clearly demonstrates the aggressive, delinquent, antisocial characteristics found in the oppositional-defiant-, conduct-disordered description provided in the DSM-III-R. Therefore, when working with children referred for acting out or disruptive behavior, the treatment will need to address the cognitive functioning of the child as well as attending to other deviant characteristics of antisocial children. Aggressive behavior includes impulsivity, poor attention control, and the inflicting of pain on others.

"Aggression" is a general term that often refers to one person inflicting pain or injury on another. Definitions of aggressive behavior presented by Berkowitz (1973) and Feshbach (1970) indicate that aggression includes intentionality. That is, the aggressor had the specific intention of hurting the victim. Others, such as Bandura (1973) and Patterson (1982), focus more on the exhibited behaviors and do not attend to the intentionality of the child. Rather than attempt to separate children's behavior by diagnostic categories presented in the DSM-III-R, Patterson (1982) reported that children's antisocial behaviors are a heterogeneous

Table 1.1. Mean T-Scores on CBCL for Referred Children.

Subscale	T Score
Somatic complaints	62
Schizoid	63
Depressed	58
Uncommunicative	59
Obsessive/compulsive	56
Social withdrawal	70
Hyperactive	72
Aggressive	75
Delinquent	70
Sum T	72
Internalizing T	67
Externalizing T	73

set of symptoms. In his extensive review of the development of coercive behavior in children, he reported that there is considerable overlap among the various dysfunctional behavior patterns that children develop. Rather than attempt to narrowly define the behavior as attention deficit disorder, oppositional defiant disorder, or conduct disorder, Patterson stated that it would be better to examine the behavior in the context of the situation and learn what conditions permit or contribute to the clinical picture.

Aggression from a social learning perspective has been generally defined as behavior that results in physical, material, or psychological injury to another person. Aggressive children demonstrate a higher rate of such behaviors as humiliating, biting, being destructive, whining, yelling, teasing, being noncompliant, and being negative than do average children. Patterson, Ray, Shaw, and Cobb (1969) reported, while conducting home observations of aggressive boys, that noncompliant behavior occurred about once every 10 minutes, and a hit or tease about every half hour.

Patterson, Reid, Jones, and Conger (1975) reported that aggressive 10- to 12-year-old children exhibited a behavior pattern typical of normal 3 year olds. Their conclusion was based on naturalistic observations conducted in the homes of aggressive and average children. They concluded that an aggressive child's process of socialization appeared to be severely inhibited and that aggressive children did not learn the social skills necessary to function effectively in their family or in peer relationships. In fact, they found that aggressive children were likely to receive three times as much punishment from their peers as nonaggressive children did (Patterson et al., 1975).

In addition to having more difficulty with peers, Patterson et al. (1975) reported that aggressive children tended to have greater difficulty mastering academic tasks, learned at a slower pace, and did not spontaneously improve without a specific intervention. Robins (1966), in an extensive follow-up study on aggressive children with poor academic skills, found that the majority experienced adjustment problems as adults.

Other studies on aggression reflected a consistency of behavior over time for aggressive children, whereas nonaggressive children tended to demonstrate a reduction in coercive behavior. Goodenough (1933) pointed out in a study on preschoolers that aggressive behavior tends to decrease as children grow older. Fawl (1963) studied an older group of children and reported the same results — that aggressive behavior tends to subside as children mature. Cairns (1979b) reported that 50% of child behavior between the ages of 1 and 2 may be classified as aggressive, but a year later only 20% of the behavior would be so classified. Patterson (1982) reported that the trend cited by Cairns is consistent with the social learning processes normal children go through as they increase prosocial behavior and decrease aggressive behavior. Aggressive children, however, did not follow this pattern. Patterson (1982), in studying normal and aggressive child behavior, reported decreases in total aversive behavior as a function of age for normal children. Children aged 2 to 4 exhibited 0.56 aversive behavior per minute, whereas the 5 to 6 year olds showed only 0.32 incident per minute. However, 11- to 12-year-old aggressive children performed aversive behaviors at approximately the rate of 2- to 4-year-old normal children, 0.68 compared to 0.56. Normal children demonstrate a significant decrease in aggressive behavior as they grow older, whereas aggressive children demonstrate a consistently high rate of aversiveness as they grow older.

In their work with disruptive children, Fleischman, Horne, and Arthur (1983) defined client identification processes and presented criteria to assist staff in evaluating children's dysfunctions. They indicated that the following characterstics are common for children often referred for treatment (Fleischman et al., 1983):

> Physical: hitting, kicking, tripping, shoving, throwing objects, and vandalizing or stealing property
> Verbal: sarcasm, criticism, "putdowns," whining, complaining, yelling, defiance, interrupting, disrupting, noncompliance
> Emotional: lack of affection, inappropriate or manipulative use of affection
> Attitudinal: negative, defeatist. (p. 6)

Fleischman et al. (1983) identified ways in which disruptive, antisocial children may be identified according to various professional labels (see Table 1.2).

Table 1.2. Labels Associated With the Identification
of Disruptive, Antisocial Children.

Professional field	Label generally used
Medical	Hyperactive, hyperkinetic
Legal-correctional	Out-of-control, child in need of supervision, incorrigible
Psychiatric	Conduct disorder, attention deficit disorder, oppositional disorder
Social work	Social deviant, antisocial, child abuse
Education	Discipline/management problem, behavior problem, emotionally handicapped (p. 7)

INCIDENCE OF BEHAVIORAL DYSFUNCTION

The aggressive behavior of problem children is a prevalent and relatively stable childhood condition which frequently requires extended therapeutic attention. Lorber and Patterson (1981) stated that approximately two thirds of the children referred for psychological evaluation and/or treatment are eventually classified as aggressive or having behavioral disorders (conduct, oppositional defiant). Patterson (1982) suggested that approximately one third of all referrals to mental health and child guidance centers are related to out-of-control or unmanageable behavior of children. There appears to be little evidence that aggressive children will simply outgrow their aggressive behavior patterns (Olweus, 1979), and in fact there is a clear indication that a large proportion of these aggressive children will need extended therapeutic assistance and/or will be incarcerated as adults (Olweus, 1976; Robins, 1966).

In a longitudinal study conducted by Gersten, Langner, Eisenberg, Simcha-Fagan, and McCarthy (1976), the onset of aggressive, antisocial behavior was reported to have an early beginning (before 6 years of age) and was predictive of continued behavior problems throughout childhood and adolescence. In their work, Gersten et al. (1976) studied 1,034 children aged 6 to 18 years and 5 years later were able to follow up 732 families (71%). On three of the six types of disturbances, specifically those tapping domains of aggression (viz., conflict with parents, delinquency, and fighting), greater or consistent levels of behavior problems were rated over time. This reflects a different trend than was true for several other factors, such as regressive anxiety, isolation, and repetitive motor behavior, which actually showed a decrease over time. For the specific cluster scores on aggression and delinquency, high correlations of stability were found. Gersten et al. (1976) noted that the conduct disorder cluster showed greater stability across time than did the neurotic cluster.

CHARACTERISTICS OF AGGRESSIVE BEHAVIOR

Olweus (1979) reviewed longitudinal studies on the stability of aggressive behavior. Sixteen studies comprising 26 independent male or mixed samples for which stability data were available were involved. Ages of subjects ranged from 2 to 18 years. His analysis consistently demonstrated the stability of aggression over time and indicated that aggressive reaction patterns observed at ages 8 and 9 could be substantially correlated with similar patterns observed 10 to 14 years later. Patterns of aggressive behavior at young ages have considerable predictive capacity for later antisocial aggression.

In order to better understand the behavior of antisocial children, a number of studies have been conducted to define characteristics of their behavior. Dodge (1980) carried out two experiments which contributed to the understanding of aggressive children's attributional tendencies. In the first study, he arranged for both aggressive and nonaggressive boys to believe that a puzzle had been rearranged by another child with a hostile, benign, or neutral intent. The hostile manipulation brought about significantly more aggression from both the aggressive and non-aggressive boys than did the benign or neutral manipulation, although the aggressive boys had a higher level of aggression than the nonaggressive boys. Patterson (1982) commented on the study:

> The findings suggest that aggressive boys may be significantly more likely to attribute hostile intent to peers in ambiguous situations. Thus, what may seem to be an unprovoked attack may relate to cue distortions. This is extremely interesting considering the extensive literature . . . showing that antisocial children are characterized in study after study as having "attentional deficits." Those studies show that these children generally do not track carefully, nor do they usually make careful discriminations. The complex interactional flow of the family or the playground would offer a rich field of possibilities for cue distortions or misattributions. Both the home and the playground are environments in which many brief, unpleasant experiences occur. They are likely to be accidental, but can easily be misconstrued as affronts or attacks. (pp. 72–73)

In a second study with the same participants (Dodge, 1980), each boy was told a story in which a peer was involved in a negative outcome for the participant, but the intention of the peer was left ambiguous. With this scenario, aggressive boys attributed hostile intentions to the peer 50% more often than nonaggressive boys. The boys who perceived hostile intentions said they would retaliate and, if the aggressive boys were led to believe the perpetrator was an aggressive peer, hostile attributions were five times greater. In a family situation, where it is likely that an aggressive child has learned that other family members are likely to be aggressive, antisocial attributions and behavior will tend to escalate quickly in a coercive cycle. Littman and Patterson (1980) reported that antisocial boys were eight times more likely than normal boys to launch "unprovoked" attacks on other family members.

In part, the work of James (1987) explained how misattributions contribute to family aggression. She studied touch patterns in families with aggressive and nonaggressive children. In families with aggressive children the percentage of touch messages between parents and their son that were understood (i.e., message intent = message received) by the family members was significantly less than the percentage of touch messages understood in functional families. The greater the dysfunction in the family, the greater the likelihood of misattribution. This finding is consistent with the study by Lochman (1987) in which he found that aggressive boys had perceptual and attributional biases operating in their social interactions. Aggressive boys minimized their perceptions of their own aggressiveness and perceived their peer partners as more aggressive than they themselves were.

In a study on families with aggressive children, P. W. Morris et al. (1988) examined parent cognitions of fathers of aggressive and well-behaved children. They found that fathers of aggressive boys perceived their family members as less concerned, supportive, and open than did fathers of well-behaved boys. Fathers of well-behaved boys perceived their families as more cohesive, more expressive, and less conflictual than did fathers of aggressive boys. These findings led the authors to speculate that a child subjected to more frequent critical evaluations by family members could develop a poorer self-image, resulting in a predisposition toward acting more aggressively, particularly in threatening interpersonal situations. A similar study by Whalen, Jessell, and Horne (1989) found that mothers of aggressive children identified themselves as victims in interactions with their aggressive children and attributed hostility to their children's behavior, whereas mothers of normal children shared responsibility for both the positive and negative aspects of their children's behavior. The previously cited research suggests that both mothers and fathers of aggressive children have considerably more negative and fewer positive thoughts about their families than do the parents of well-behaved children. Patterson (1980), through home observations, has identified the mother as the victim in many aggressive interactions within the family, and his behavioral measures confirm the beliefs expressed by mothers in the Whalen et al. (1989) study. Therefore, it appears that parental cognitions and perceptions must be altered during treatment if behavioral change, maintenance, and generalization are to occur.

Chapter 2
Understanding Antisocial Behavior

FOUR CASES FOR TREATMENT

Antisocial behavior takes a variety of forms and shapes. Four cases referred for treatment reflect the diversity of situations that may be encountered in clinical settings.

Bobby

Bobby, a 12 year old , was initially referred by Child Protective Services. He had been removed from his parents' home as a result of abuse and neglect. Bobby's father was incarcerated in the county jail for burglary, and his mother had been arrested on prostitution charges as she attempted to raise bail money for the father. The home had no heat, running water, or electricity. Bobby had two siblings, one older and one younger, and they too had been placed in foster care, although with other foster families. The initial referral was to assist the foster parents in child management concerns for Bobby.

Bobby was in a class for severely emotionally disturbed children and had been evaluated by a school psychologist who reported a full-scale WISC-R IQ of 72. He reported the score probably was not reflective of Bobby's intelligence level because Bobby had been very uncooperative, refusing to participate in much of the evaluation process. The teacher completed a classroom observation form which indicated that Bobby was out of his seat often, talked frequently, and was in many ways a highly disturbing element in the classroom. Her evaluation was that Bobby was much too bright to be in a class with slow learners, but that because of his behavior pattern there were no other classes appropriate for him. She reported that Bobby was the worst behavioral problem in the class of six students and that he often fought both in the classroom and on the playground, frequently took items that belonged to other students or to the school, and lied and cursed with abandon. She also observed that he was cute, friendly, and, for brief moments, could be one of the most lovable students with whom she had worked.

The foster parents reported that Bobby was the biggest problem they had ever encountered in their 20 years of foster parent work. He would lie, steal, curse, fight, argue, and run away from home almost daily. His temper tantrums would be unexpected and explosive, at times resulting in damage to household items or walls, doors, and even Bobby's personal possessions. While quite small for his age, he would have to be physically restrained at times because of feared danger to himself or to others. They reported, though, that he was also the most lovable child they had had in their home and that at times he could be a most helpful, friendly, courteous, and respectful person. One concern of the foster parents was that they had been instructed by Child Protective Services (CPS) to not use corporal punishment. They had always agreed in previous cases, but they didn't believe they had the skills to discipline Bobby without spankings. In fact, Bobby would frequently seem to deliberately get in trouble and then ask the foster parents to spank him. When they wouldn't, he would engage in a temper tantrum until they would have to physically restrain him.

During the initial interview with Bobby he presented as a cute, smiling, and extremely cooperative student. He fully cooperated with the interviewer, answering questions and participating in a helpful manner. He appeared considerably brighter than his tested score represented and did not appear to have the social problems reported by the teacher and the foster parents. When informed that the purpose of the interview was not to certify that he should be sent back to his family, but to learn about him and to find ways to help his foster parents work more effectively with him, he began a temper tantrum that resulted in his having to be physically restrained to prevent damage to himself and to the equipment and room. From then on he was most uncooperative and belligerent, often cursing and attempting to run away from the interview room.

Johnni

Johnni, a 14-year-old seventh grader, was referred by CPS because her mother had beaten her following an argument. The argument had developed because of a school contact in which it was reported that Johnni had stolen items from other students and had been in several fights at school. Child Protective Services, in conjunction with the juvenile court, wanted treatment for Johnni in order to alter the behavior pattern she had demonstrated since entering school. Johnni's mother reported that she had been difficult to work with since she was a baby, was argumentative, fought a lot even as a preschooler, was sullen and insolent, and was very irresponsible. In recent months Johnni had been caught shoplifting and had been taken to the juvenile center. She had also been caught in several acts of vandalism in the community, including damaging a neighbor's car. There was no father in the home.

Johnni's school presented a profile similar to that reported by her mother. Her school record showed behavioral problems going back to the first grade. She was often in fights, frequently refused to participate in school activities, including not doing homework assignments, did not cooperate in school fuctions, and was often unmanageable on the playground and in the cafeteria. When evaluated by a school psychologist, Johnni was defined as low average in intelligence, with too little deficiency to warrant special placement, although she was marginal. Johnni met early guidelines for a learning-disabled placement in that she was functioning more than two grades below class level, but she had never been placed in remedial classes.

When Johnni was interviewed, she seemed very disengaged from the process. She appeared to be insolent and angry and was noncooperative. She reported that there was nothing wrong with her and that she just wished people would leave her alone. She attributed her problems to people being nosy and interfering in her life. Johnni also reported that most of the victims of her aggression deserved to be victims, that they had deserved the trouble she gave them. She demonstrated no remorse concerning her actions but seemed put out that she had to answer for her behavior. She said that her peer group, many members of which had also been in trouble at home, in the community, and at school, was the most important part of her life, and that her mother should leave her alone to do as she pleased because she was old enough to take care of herself. She reported that she was sexually active and that she had experimented with alcohol and marijuana, but that what she did with her body was no one's business.

Candy

Candy had been reported to CPS by her teacher because she had come to school with several large bruises on her body. She was 12 years old and in the seventh grade. There were no problems reported at school, and her academic records indicated that, although she was not a star student, she was a good, average achiever. Teachers reported her as being quiet but friendly and somewhat shy.

The mother and stepfather reported that Candy had been quite good as a young child. The mother had divorced when Candy was a pre-schooler and had remarried when Candy was in the second grade. Candy and her new stepfather never seemed to get along well. Candy had usually refused to mind him, and as she got older the arguments between the two became more heated and violent. It was the stepfather who apparently had inflicted the bruises on her.

Candy reported she enjoyed school but that she hated her home life. She said she couldn't stand to live with her stepfather and that she would never cooperate with him. She said he was rude, crude, and offensive in the way he dressed, ate, and behaved around the home. Further, Candy said she would run away from home rather than continue to live with him.

Billy

Billy was referred by his school and his parents. He was a bright sixth grader who was in accelerated placement classes. He had been recognized early as very intellectually capable and had progressed rapidly in his academic skills. He had few effective interpersonal skills, however, and was often in trouble at school and with his peers. Billy particularly liked to tease other students, to show off about how smart he was, and to criticize the work of others. He also liked to take on teachers and would look for opportunities to make fun of them in front of the class or to adults. He served as the class clown and would disrupt activities and call attention to himself by doing outlandish things such as wearing flowing capes and broad-brimmed hats to class, turning animals loose in the classroom, setting fires in the closet, and engaging in other highly disruptive behaviors, although he usually avoided physical fights or altercations.

Billy's parents reported equally disruptive behavior at home. They had always found him to be bright and advanced for his age and assumed he would outgrow the disruptive behavior patterns. However, as he grew older, he became considerably more difficult around the home and regularly questioned his parents' authority over him. The parents reported considerable marital difficulty and attributed much of the responsibility for their problems to Billy, stating that dealing with him took so much energy that there was little left over for the adults to share in their time together.

During the interview Billy treated the behavioral problems mostly as a joke and reported he thought it was funny that adults couldn't handle him. He said he thought they were too slow to keep up with him and that he didn't respect people who couldn't cope with his antics. He showed no sense of responsibility for his actions toward others.

EXPLANATIONS FOR
ANTISOCIAL BEHAVIOR

There are a number of theorectical explanations for the occurrence of antisocial behavior. These include biological, sociological, and psychological emphases, with the psychological emphasis further divided into several models. The following section provides a brief account of how various models explain why some children develop antisocial behavior.

Instinctual Theories

A historical review of the interpretations of aggressive behavior shows that instinctual theory (e.g., Freud), has been prominent. Early psychological theories tended to interpret human behavior as being primarily a function of instinctual forces. Bandura (1973) stated that, in general, instinctual explanations of aggression are based on the belief that people are innately endowed with an aggressive drive. Within this context, two theories of aggression are of primary importance: the psychoanalytic instinctual theory of Freud and the ethological theory of Lorenz.

Freud (1920, 1959) believed that human behavior is largely determined by oppositional interplay of the life (Eros) and the death (Thanatos) instincts. The life instincts are directed at the enhancement and continuation of life, whereas the death instincts continually seek to destroy the organism. The death instinct's function is to return the organism to its original inanimate form.

According to Zillman (1979), the most remarkable aspect of Freud's death instinct is that Freud considered it to be directed against the self. Self-destruction, however, is prevented by the life instinct which serves to divert the destructive drive from the self to others (Frued, 1959). In Freud's view the death instinct forces the individual to direct aggressive actions toward the social and/or physical environment in order to save him or herself from self-destruction. Consequently, interpersonal aggression is derived from self-aggression rather than being a primary force in and of itself.

To Freud, aggression satisfies an instinctual predisposition and is therefore inevitable. Humans cannot escape their aggressive, violent tendencies and, in fact, if these violent tendencies were successfully controlled, total self-destruction would result. This is not to say, however, that the intensity of aggression and its form of expression are unmodifiable. Freud (1959) suggested that the development of emotional ties between people can alter extreme destructiveness, as can providing opportunities for outward release of the aggressive impulse. Gillespie (1971) suggested that most contemporary psychoanalysts continue to view aggression as an instinctual drive but reject the self-destructive death instinct.

Lorenz (1964) proposed an ethological explanation of aggression which, like Freud's, is based on the idea that people have an instinctual system that produces aggressive energy independent of external stimulation. Megargee and Hokanson (1970) suggested that where the theorists differ is in their views of the nature of inhibitory influences. Lorenz believed that inhibitions have evolved and must therefore have a biological basis, whereas Freud contended that inhibitions develop in the process of interacting with the environment and that the primary inhibitory agent in the individual is the superego.

According to Lorenz (1964, 1966), if the instinctual aggressive energy is not released through aggressive action, it will gradually increase to a point where it will force out aggressive behavior with or without appropriate environmental stimuli. Therefore, the aggressive energy buildup is of a self-perpetuating nature and it is inevitable that aggression will occur.

Zillman (1979) reduced the ethological model of aggression to the following three propositions:

1. Aggressive energy is produced spontaneously and continually at a constant rate within the organism.
2. The evocation of aggressive behavior is a joint function of the amount of accumulated aggressive energy available and the strength of aggression-releasing stimuli impinging on the organism.
3. The specific manifestations of aggression and the intensity of evoked behaviors are largely a function of the amount of prevailing aggressive behavior.

The ethological view of aggression, therefore, is that it is inevitable, yet modifiable, because releases of aggressive energy will presumably serve to prevent the growth needed for major aggressive outbursts. If aggressive energy is prevented from accumulating to higher and higher levels, dangerous aggressive outbrusts cannot occur because they generally require large amounts of energy.

Drive Theory Explanations of Aggression

During the mid-twentieth century, the aggressive drive perspective of aggression became popular. In 1939, Dollard, Doob, Miller, Mowrer, and Sears published their work on the frustration-aggression hypothesis of aggressive behavior. These theorists believed that people are motivated to behave aggressively by a frustration-produced drive rather than by an instinctual aggressive force. This hypothesis gained widespread acceptance during the past four decades as it was formulated by Dollard, Doob, Miller, Mowrer, and Sears (1939) and later expanded on (Feshbach, 1964, 1970; Sears, Whiting, Nowlis, & Sears, 1953; Whiting & Child, 1953).

According to the frustration-aggression hypothesis, interference with goal-directed activity leads to an aggressive drive which motivates behavior designed to injure or destroy the person toward whom it is directed. Infliction of such an injury is then assumed to reduce the aggressive drive (Bandura, 1973).

In its initial form, this hypothesis stated that (a) frustration always produces aggression and (b) aggression is always a consequence of frustration (Dollard et al., 1939). Many individuals have erroneously interpreted the statement, "Aggression is always a consequence of frustration," to mean that frustration always leads to overt displays of aggression. Consequently, Miller (1941) clarified the point by postulating that instigation to aggression inevitably follows frustration, but whether instigation is actually expressed depends on the relative strengths of instigation and inhibition. In this revised form of the frustration-aggression hypothesis, frustration was seen as necessary but not sufficient for the occurrence of aggression.

Zillman (1979) pointed out that Dollard et al. (1939) specified that the motivational strength toward aggression was a function of the reinforcement value of the frustrated goal response, the degree of frustation of this goal response, and the number of frustrated response sequences. Frustrations are then maintained within the individual and continue to accumulate until they reach a level at which an act that would otherwise be tolerable evokes aggression.

The inhibition of aggression is also related to time in that the lack of immediate overt manifestations of aggression leads to prolonged covert consequences that eventually occur in a different form (Zillman, 1979). It was thought that the strength of the inhibition was directly related to the severity of punishment anticipated for exhibiting aggressive behavior. Bandura (1969), in fact, found that punishment exerted a regulatory function over aggressive behavior. The idea of catharsis in frustration-aggression theory is then generally equated with the reduction in inhibition of the instigation to aggression. For Dollard et al. (1939), this reduction was achieved at least in part by any and every act of aggression. The drive toward aggression is therefore increased by frustration and decreased by catharsis.

Several attempts have been made to modify the frustration-aggression hypothesis to accommodate emerging research (Barker, Dembo, & Lewin, 1941; Berkowitz, 1962, 1965, 1969; Feshbach, 1970; Maier, 1949). One attempt at modification that has received attention during the past two decades has been the work of Berkowitz (1965). Berkowitz proposed that frustration induces an emotional reaction (e.g., anger) that creates a readiness for only aggressive acts and that aggressive responses will not occur, even given this readiness, unless there are suitable cues. Berkowitz (1965) also posited that objects having some connection with aggression may have the capacity to serve as cues in eliciting an aggressive response. With the exception of Berkowitz's point on objects connected with aggression, Zillman (1979) stated that the revision to a large extent rephrased the frustration-aggression hypothesis as amended by Miller (1941, 1948). Emotional anger and aggression readiness replaced the earlier concepts of aggressive drive and repsonse strength for aggression, whereas stimulus dependence (Dollard et al., 1939) was similarly stressed by Berkowitz. The concept of suitable cues then constitutes a unique contribution to the revised frustration-aggression hypothesis of Berkowitz (1965).

In comparison, the instinctual and drive theories differ according to the innate versus externally stimulated motivational forces of aggression but are similar in terms of their implications for the regulation of aggressive behavior. Both perspectives acknowledge a continuous source of aggressive energy which requires periodic release and assume that aggression is reduced by behaving aggressively (Bandura, 1973; Feshbach, 1970).

Until recently, human behavior was largely depicted by personality theories as being instigated by the inner motivational forces of drives, impulses, and needs which often operated below the level of consciousness (Bandura, 1977). Furthermore, the major aim of aggression was considered to be the pleasure or satisfaction gained from inflicting injury and/or destruction. According to Bandura (1973), however, explanations emphasizing instigators of frustration and destructive aims have very limited explanatory power.

Learning Theory Explanations of Aggression

Learning theoretical perspectives offer several explanations of aggressive behavior. Scott (1958) addressed the instrumental learning of aggression and stated that the motivation for fighting is strongly increased by success, and that the longer success continues, the stronger the motivation becomes. Therefore, Scott's ideas can be translated as indicating that the likelihood that aggression will occur increases as aggression is reinforced (Zillman, 1979). Other learning theory interpretations of aggression are seen in relationship to the stimulus control of aggression. The environmental stimuli that precede reinforcement are seen as having a potential capability for controlling behavior. These environmental cues serve as discriminate stimuli that help the individual respond as indicated by the prevailing contingencies of reinforcement or punishment.

According to Zillman (1979), Berkowitz has always entertained what could be considered a stimulus-control theory of aggression (1962, 1965) and has recently committed himself more explicitly to the paradigm of classical conditioning of aggressive responses and to stimulus control in general (Berkowitz, 1970, 1973, 1974).

Among learning theory explanations of aggression, there are also those that acknowledge genetic predispositions and biological, anatomical, and physiological components (Eron, 1980). Patterson (1982), for example, has reviewed research related to inherited antisocial characteristics of people and reports that research findings support a genetic predispostion for aggressiveness in some animal species. He cites the work of Mednick and Christiansen (1977) which reported the hyporeactivity of adult and juvenile criminals toward aversive stimuli, and of Mednick and Hutchings (1977) who found that there was a relationship between antisocial behavior of the child and criminality of the father. Their studies on identical and fraternal twins suggest a genetic contribution to antisocial functioning. Although there may be differences among species and there may be an innate predisposition toward aggression in some situations, Patterson (1982) states:

> The literature suggests that species differ in the (innate) disposition to learn aggression. For the animal lacking social experience, aggressive behavior may be expressed in an incomplete form. Skill in aggression requires additional learning. The form in which aggressive behavior is expressed may also change as a function of age. For example, its earliest manifestations in primates may be temper tantrums, which do not have to be learned. (p. 134)

The underlying assumption is that aggressive behavior is indeed learned, but that genetic and hereditary components also have a bearing. However, the learning aspects are extremely important and can ordinarily overcome whatever natural or constitutional dispositions there are toward aggression.

Currently, and for much of the past 20 years, social learning principles and techniques have been implemented in the treatment and conceptualization of the aggressive population. Social learning theory approaches the explanation of human behavior in terms of a continuous reciprocal interaction among three areas: "Human functioning is explained in terms of a model of triadic reciprocality in which behavior, cognitive and other personal factors, and environmental events all operate as interacting determinants of each other" (Bandura, 1986, p. 18). The social learning theory of aggression outlines ways aggressive behavior patterns are developed (origins), what provokes people to behave aggressively (instigators), and what maintains their aggressive actions (reinforcers).

Aggressive behavior, according to social learning theory, is acquired through learning in a social context, either from direct experience or by observing the behavior of other people. Fleischman, Horne, and Arthur (1983) state that

> the problem behavior of the individual is neither illogical or crazy; rather it is seen as a pattern of learned responses to the contingencies of that system. Furthermore, while the behavior of others within the system contributes to the individual's deviancy, the behavior of the individual contributes to and maintains the behaviors of others toward the person. (p. 19)

Thus, although biological factors may influence aggressive behavior, children are not born predisposed to perform specific aggressive acts (Bandura, 1973).

Of primary concern to social learning theory is the role of modeling. Although new forms of aggressive behavior can be shaped by selective reinforcement of successive approximations to it, most complex behavior is acquired by observing the behavior of models. For children, behavior may be patterned after the people they observe in everyday life or after characters they become acquainted with via reading or television. A distinction is made, however, between the direct and vicarious learning that contributes to the acquisition of aggressive behavior and factors that influence whether the child will actually use the aggressive behavior he or she has acquired (Bandura, 1973). Therefore, social learning theory pays a great deal of attention to the potential models that serve as reinforcers for both prosocial and antisocial behaviors.

The maintenance of aggressive behavior is largely dependent on the consequences of an aggressive act. Aggressive behaviors that are rewarded tend to be repeated, whereas those that are punished or receive a less than expected reward tend to be discarded. The kinds of reinforcement that strengthen aggression are variable and include vicarious or observed reinforcement. Substantial evidence is available to support the importance of reinforcement in shaping and maintaining aggressive behavior (Bandura, 1973, 1977, 1986).

A basic idea within social learning theory is that people strive to maximize rewards while minimizing costs (Horne, 1982). It is believed that social relationships that are maintained are so maintained by achieving a high ratio of rewards to costs and thus are seen as satisfactory. Conflict develops when rewards or behavior-maintaining contingencies do not exist or when faulty behavior change efforts are implemented. This idea of exchange is further identified by the processes of reciprocity and coercion (Patterson & Hops, 1972). "Reciprocity" refers to social exchanges in which two people positively reinforce each other at an equitable rate to maintain their relationship. Conversely, "coercion" refers to a relationship in which a person provides aversive reactions that control the behavior of the other. In this case, negative reinforcement is the result of termination of the aversiveness.

To date, reinforcement and punishment have been emphasized as constructs that significantly influence the occurrence of behavior patterns. Within social learning theory there has been a growing emphasis on the role of thoughts, feelings, and other more complex cognitive events in controlling human behavior (Bandura, 1986; Fleischman et al., 1983). This theoretical and clinical approach provides a more complete framework within which to assess and treat oppositional defiant and conduct disorders of children.

Childhood Aggression and Child Abuse

Recent work on our Family Therapy Research Project, particularly by Glaser (1989), has explored the similarities between abusive families and distressed families (clinic-referred families with oppositional-defiant- or conduct-disordered children, but without abuse). Parallel research in the areas of child abuse and childhood aggression is taking place, but findings from the two areas have not been integrated well. Child abuse studies and child aggression studies may be describing the same children, or there may be considerable overlap, which suggests that research groups must be much more carefully described than has been true in the past.

At present, social learning theory in the area of child abuse may be described as a social interactional model of child abuse. The social interactional model has evolved from a long tradition of person-environment psychology (Cairns, 1979a, 1979c; Ekehammar, 1974). In order to illustrate the social interactional model, Wolfe (1985) compared it with the psychiatric model. He noted that the psychiatric model has conceptualized child abuse as a distinct personality syndrome or disorder in which parental psychopathology is viewed as being responsible for child abuse (Melnick & Hurley, 1969; Oates, 1979; Sloane & Meier, 1983). Psychiatric model studies comparing abusive with nonabusive parents have focused on measuring psychological problems such as self-esteem, depression, and impulse control. Early childhood experiences, coping and defense mechanisms, personality profiles, and similar characteristics have also been examined within the context of the psychiatric model

(Wolfe, 1985). On the other hand, the social interactional model emphasizes the bidirectional influences of behavior among family members, antecedent events that may precipitate abuse, and consequences that may maintain the use of excessive punishment with the child (Burgess, 1978; Burgess & Richardson, 1984). Of major interest to social interactional researchers is the current behavior of the abusive or distressed parent in the context of the family and the community. Also of interest are the parents' learning history, interpersonal experience, and intrinsic capabilities.

Within the social interactional model research has focused on the microanalysis of interactions among family members with the expectation that abusive parents would display rates and patterns of abusive behavior distinguishing them from nonabusive parents. In the area of childhood aggression, the target child and other members of the family are viewed as active participants in an escalating cycle of coercion (Patterson, 1982; Reid, Tapline, & Lorber, 1981). Whether or not parents become abusive is seen as a function of their aggregate (a) childbearing and interpersonal skills and (b) the frequency and intensity of aversive stimulation impinging on family members from the outside or within the family unit (Burgess, 1978). These correlates of abuse do not cause abuse. It is hypothesized that child-aversive behavior and a stress-filled environment interact with parental experience and competence to give rise to the mediating variable(s) of conditioned arousal and/or negative attributions that in turn lead to aggressive retaliation (Knutson, 1978; Vasta, 1982). Social interactional researchers have focused on abusive parents' emotional and cognitive reactions to aversive child stimuli and the interactional patterns of abusive families (Wolfe, 1985).

Wolfe (1985) reported that abusive parents were significantly more punitive and harsh toward their children than nonabusive parents in child-rearing situations. He noted that data concerning aversive parent–child interactions have been alternately interpreted: Proponents of the psychiatric model interpret aversive interactions as indicative of pronounced impulse disorder or characterological defect on the part of the abusive parents. On the other hand, social interaction theorists argue that abusive parents fail to use contingencies that would reduce child behavior problems. They also fail to use positive approaches to teach their children desirable behaviors. The result is a cycle of aversive behavior that may culminate in harm to the child (Kelly, 1983; Wolfe, Kaufman, Aragona, & Sandler, 1981).

The psychiatric and the social interaction models are not mutually exclusive viewpoints. Both attempt to understand individual characteristics of abusive parents in relation to prior experience and current demands. The major distinction lies in the focus on the parent as the principal cause of the abuse. How the role of the parent is conceptualized affects the types of questions asked by researchers and the selection of interventions by therapists.

The social interactional model assumes that parents who abuse their children display behaviors belonging to the same general response class as aggression. Wolfe (1985) noted that a key factor in explaining interpersonal violence is the transition from anger to aggression. He provided a parallel explanation of aggression theory and child abuse as follows:

> Hostile aggression in humans appears to be highly attributable to situational cues and characteristics of the individual (Averill, 1983; Berkowitz, 1983; Zillman, 1979). In the case of abusive parents, the situational cues involve aversive behavior or features of the child, and the presumed individual characteristics include such factors as oversensitivity (Knutson, 1978), disinhibition of aggression (Zillman, 1979), poor skill repertoire (Novaco, 1978), and related characteristics of the adult. Experiments with normal subjects have determined that anger, a precursor to aggression, is a highly interpersonal emotion that typically involves a close affectional relationship between the angry person and the target (Averill, 1983). To explain how anger may lead to aggression, Berkowitz (1983) maintained that the paired association of noxious events (such as child tantrums) with otherwise neutral stimuli (such as child's facial expression) can evoke aggressive responding in the adult in subsequent interactions. Presumably, the adult is responding to cues that have previously been associated with frustration or anger, and the adult's behavior toward the child may be potentiated by these conditioning experiences (Berkowitz, 1983; Vasta, 1982). (p. 475)

Abusive families and distressed families (clinic families referred for child behavior problems) have aggression in common, and several studies have used distressed parents as a comparison group with abusive parents (Lahey, Conger, Atkeson, & Teiber, 1984; Lorber, Felton, & Reid, 1984; Wolfe & Mosk, 1983). Distressed and abusive families are thought to have similar coercive interactions between parents and among parents and children. Thus marital variables (e.g., marital conflict, spouse abuse) seem to be salient for both groups. In both distressed and abusive families, the parent and the child are more likely to reciprocate aversive behavior and to maintain higher levels of conflict than in normal families.

Patterson (1986) presented three interlocking structural equation models focusing on three characteristics of antisocial children: (a) children do not outgrow antisocial problems; (b) antisocial problems covary with a myriad of other problems such as academic failure, rejection by peers, and possible low self-esteem; and (c) antisocial children have parents who lack family management skills. He suggested that these three characteristics define different stages of the same process.

Fundamental to Patterson's model is the coercive process. The coercive process is the theoretical suggestion that parents of conduct-disordered children are trapped in many different types of negative relationships and life experiences. It specifically refers to the aversive interchanges between aggressive children and their parents. In effect, it has been observed that maternal reprimands (apparently aversive stimuli) seem to serve as positive reinforcers for some children.

Patterson (1982) suggested that a mediating variable for antisocial behavior in children consists of disruptions in family management skills. Family management skills include (a) clearly stated house rules, (b) parental monitoring of child behavior, (c) parental sanctions (providing consequences contingently), and (d) problem solving (e.g., crisis management, negotiating compromises). Disruptions in family management skills are due to a deficit in problem-solving skills.

Research in our project suggests that the separate tracks of conduct disorder research and child abuse research may be overlooking the fact that samples of conduct-disordered children and abused children may overlap or often even be the same (Glaser, 1989). Many of the needs of aggressive and abusive families overlap, and treatment for both groups takes a similar form. Wolfe (1985) recommends that every community offer programs to reduce situational demands on parents and develop programs to help increase parental competence. Respite homes and relief parents could provide temporary relief for child-related demands. More stable provisions for relieving child distress include subsidized day care and preschool for families, volunteer homemaker programs that provide nonthreatening, paraprofessional treatment, and early stimulation programs for enhancing the child's abilities in such areas as language and social interaction. With regard to prevention of family violence there should be attempts to teach alternatives to violence, to promote the affective quality of family relationships, and to encourage the inhibition of anger in aggressive ways.

Glaser (1989) has suggested that intervention programs address parent and child cognitive styles, specifically parent attributions of child behavior and child attributions of parent behavior. In addition to teaching parents anger control, stress management, and parental competency skills, children should be taught ways of interacting and solving problems with their parents. Part of this includes learning how to minimize the eliciting of aversive parent behavior by children. Of course, the best way to teach this is in context. As a result, therapists, counselors, and paraprofessionals can have the opportunity to observe, model, and intervene in parent–child interactions. Finally, family environment, especially level of conflict within the home, cannot be ignored by any form of intervention. A systemic approach is recommended, namely, addressing marital or spousal conflict, conflict with authorities or government agencies, social isolation problems, and poverty.

Chapter 3
Treatment Programs

There are a significant number of children and adolescents in need of mental health services. Kazdin (1988), in reviewing the extent of mental health problems of children, reported that approximately 9 million, as many as 15% of all children, are in need of mental health services. While the need is there, the majority of children needing attention have not received it, for Bahm, Chandler, and Eisenberg (1961) reported that only a small fraction of the children referred for treatment actually receive an offer of services. Kazdin (1988) reported that only 20 to 33% of children with significant dysfunctions actually obtain treatment.

Of the children who are identified as being in need of treatment and who actually receive it, a large proportion, perhaps as many as two thirds, are conduct or oppositional-defiant-disordered (Lorber & Patterson, 1981). Roach (1958) reported that nearly one third of all referrals by teachers and parents for mental health services were for children who were identified as out of control or unmanageable within the school and home. Twenty-five years later, Patterson (1982) reported a similar finding, that approximately one third of all referrals to mental health and child guidance centers relate to out-of-control or unmanageable behavior of children. Levitt (1971) reported that of those who did seek mental health services and were accepted for treatment, the treatment offered typically was individual traditional therapy that resulted in little help for socially aggressive children. Treatment of the individual child by traditional methods left much to be desired in terms of effecting a lasting change in inappropriate behaviors of children in the home and school (Meltzoff & Kornreich, 1970; Teuber & Powers, 1953). In his historical overview of the effectiveness of child psychotherapy, Kazdin (1988) cited a number of studies that questioned the efficacy of early treatment for children.

Traditional therapies for treating antisocial children have been based on verbal expressive modes that seek to unbind the inexpressive, emotionally repressed individual. However, the techniques developed are not relevant for children who are already very expressive and without a commitment to social expectations. In recent years, treatment programs specifically designed for working with conduct- and oppositional-defiant-disordered children have been developed with research support for their efficacy.

APPROACHES TO TREATMENT

Treatment of oppositional-defiant-, conduct-disordered children has taken a variety of forms. Keat (1979) developed a multimodel treatment emphasizing a variety of methods to use, depending on the nature and extent of the problem. Hoghughi, Lyons, Muckley, and Swainston (1988) described various child problems and developed a taxonomy of treatment methods for addressing them. For behaviors indicative of antisocial children they list a series of treatments, including parent training, seeking help from specialists, contingency contracting, positive reinforcement, counseling, family therapy, and therapeutic communities.

Psychopharmacology has also been used as an approach or an adjunct to treatment of antisocial children, but the results have not been promising. Gittelman and Kanner (1986), in summarizing research on psychopharmacology with antisocial children, report:

> In summary, there is no well-established pharmacotherapy of conduct disorders except for the single satisfactory study of lithium . . . . Further research is required to provide clear estimates of drug efficacy in children with pure conduct disorders and in those who also suffer from ADDH [Attention Deficit Disorder–Hyperactivity] or from depression (p. 474)

Institutional placement has also been examined as a treatment approach for antisocial children, and although the immediate impact of residential treatment seems to alter behavior, in long-term effectiveness it has not proven to be an improvement over other approaches. Quay (1986b) reviewed research related to residential treatment and summarized the findings:

> Although there is ample evidence for the effectiveness of residential treatment to bring about in-program behavior change, there is little, if any, evidence for lasting change deriving from any of the differing intervention modalities that have been studied. Progess, if any, in the last six to eight years is almost nonexistent. Yet residential placement, if not treatment, is clearly here to stay, if only for the limited number of children and adolescents who are clearly dangerous to themselves or, more likely, to others. (p. 578)

Quay's findings are consistent with the present authors' personal experience working with a residential correctional treatment program for 7 years. The program seemed to be effective for developing educational improvements and behavior change, but the long-term impact appeared to be negligible.

Educational interventions have also been popular for helping children to change. While a number of programs and approaches have been described, a review of intervention programs as summarized by MacMillan and Kavale (1986), reported that several programs have been effective in helping to change antisocial behavior within the school environment, but that none of the approaches scored high on extended effectiveness:

> This analysis shows that the behavioral model rates highly on all criteria except extended effectiveness. The low rating on this criterion may account for the fact that the behavioral model has been included in a majority of educational programs but rarely as a total program. [This] suggests that behavioral interventions must be incorporated into another model for maximum effectiveness . . . . Consequently, behavioral interventions are often the major means of behavior management in a total intervention system that takes an eclectic approach. (p. 611)

With effective treatment programs, broad-spectrum behavioral intervention has demonstrated an impact in a variety of ways, including school, family, group, individual, and institutional programs.

SOCIAL LEARNING FAMILY THERAPY INTERVENTIONS

Downing (1983) and Horne (1982) have reported that the social learning approach to helping families with aggressive children is promising and, given its viewpoint that family concerns result primarily from the learning patterns within the family system, the model seems to be an appropriate conceptualization. Bandura (1977) concluded that family members' goals, relationship patterns, and behaviors are not genetically acquired, nor do they usually result from organic dysfunctions or injuries. Rather, the patterns are learned and consequently are alterable.

Historically, behaviorally oriented therapists have developed systematic treatment programs while placing a strong emphasis on empirical evaluation and validation of treatment outcome. Accordingly, these therapists assume that behavior and interactions are controlled, shaped, and maintained by environmental events and can be changed by the modification of these environmental contingencies. Dysfunctional behavior is conceptualized primarily as the result of inconsistent and coercive methods of control which, when altered, serve to change the unwanted behavior (Kniskern & Gurman, 1981). The social learning treatment of the antisocial child has generally taken two forms, parent training and behavioral or social learning family therapy.

Parent Training

The development of the social learning approach to treating antisocial children has been documented in several sources (Horne, 1982; Horne & Patterson, 1980; O'Dell, 1974; Patterson, 1982; Patterson, Reid, Jones, & Conger, 1975). During the late 1960s and early 1970s researchers established that training parents in the use of behavioral principles and methods could be effective in altering the behavior of children with conduct problems. Placing parents in the role of teachers is an appealing approach because parents can learn skills not only for solving current problems, but also, it is hoped, they will learn to prevent future difficulties (McAuley, 1982). Explanations of the development of conduct disorders suggest that aggressive behaviors are shaped and maintained by positive and negative reinforcers delivered through child–adult or child–child interactions. It follows therefore that the emphasis in treatment has been on teaching parents to alter their behavior toward their children (Gross, 1983).

The predominant work with parent training for families with aggressive children has been conducted at the Oregon Social Learning Center (OSLC) under athe direction of Gerald Patterson and John Reid. The early work of the OSLC staff members centered on the application of social learning principles to the training of parents and others in the child's environment to act as agents of change. In the mid-1960s the OSLC staff began efforts to develop an empirically based low-cost treatment approach for families of aggressive and predelinquent youth. A second parent-training program of note was that developed by Constance Hanf at the University of Oregon Medical School designed specifically to treat child noncompliance. This program has subsequently been modified by Rex Forehand and his associates at the University of Georgia (Forehand & McMahon, 1981).

The parent-training program devised by Patterson and his colleagues consists of three stages. Movement from one stage to the next is contingent on successful completion of the preceding stage. The three stages are (a) learning the concepts of behavioral theory, (b) learning to define deviant behavior and monitoring and recording its occurrence, and (c) learning to modify one or two of the child's problematic behaviors (Patterson et al., 1975). Consequently, once these three stages have been accomplished, further training can be utilized to address other child behavior concerns.

Several initial studies on the application of Patterson's approach were undertaken. The first major application of social learning theory to treatment of the aggressive-child population occurred between 1968 and 1972. During that time Patterson treated 27 boys and their families (Patterson,

1974, 1975). Home observations showed that approximately two thirds of the boys experienced at least a 30% reduction in 44 aggressive behaviors. Additionally, parents' daily reports showed a 50% decrease in the aversive behaviors of concern to them. Follow-up data indicated that the improvements were maintained up to 12 months after termination of treatment (Arnold, Levine, & Patterson, 1975). Further refinements in the treatment program provided for the addition of control measures necessary to conduct comparative clinical research, with the results continuing to demonstrate the effectiveness of behavioral parent-training approaches (Walter & Gilmore, 1973; Wiltz & Patterson, 1974). Replication studies have been conducted (Fleischman, 1981; Fleischman & Horne, 1979; Patterson & Hops, 1972; Patterson, Ray, Shaw, & Cobb, 1969; Patterson & Reid, 1973) that provide support for this model.

Despite the positive effects reported, several other investigators were either partially or totally unable to replicate the findings (Eyberg & Johnson, 1974; Johnson & Christensen, 1975). Fleischman (1981) responded to these discrepancies with a complete replication of the original study. Once again, the findings of Patterson were repeated, giving credence to the notion that perhaps the variables associated with the application of social learning technology (viz., therapist experience, program organization and delivery, client characteristics, length of treatment) must also be assessed. The findings of Patterson's earlier studies were also supported by a multivariate analysis of these same data by Horne and Van Dyck (1983) that showed maintenance and generalization of treatment effects.

In a discussion of the results of the OSLC program, Patterson (1982) strongly suggested that consistent outcome success requires a combination of parent-training technology and skills for dealing with client resistance, marital conflict, and family crises.

In an ongoing project at the University of Georgia, over 100 mother-child pairs referred for noncompliance and other behavior problems had participated in treatment by 1984, spanning a period of approximately 10 years (Forehand, Furey, & McMahon, 1984). Over the course of that period, three stages of treatment development had become apparent: (a) demonstrating the short-term effects of the program (b) evaluating the generality of the program, and (c) examining ways to enhance the generality of treatment effects.

Generally, the results of the research conducted at the University of Georgia have revealed the following information: (a) The parent-training program effectively modifies selected parent behaviors and child noncompliance in clinic settings (Forehand & King, 1974, 1977); (b) These changes have generalized over time, settings, behavior, and siblings (Forehand et al., 1979; Humphreys, Forehand, McMahon, & Roberts,

1978; Peed, Roberts, & Forehand, 1977; Wells, Forehand, & Griest, 1980; Wells, Griest, & Forehand, 1980); and (c) Teaching parents self-control techniques and a thorough knowledge of social learning principles enhances generalizability (McMahon, Forehand, & Griest, 1981). Although the studies attest to the effect of generalizability, Baum and Forehand (1981) observed that only six studies reported behavioral observation data for groups of subjects 8 months or more following the completion of treatment.

In an effort to determine the extent of this treatment's effectiveness, Baum and Forehand (1981) examined the long-term effects of the parent-training program at the University of Georgia. Results indicated that posttreatment gains were maintained or improved at periods of up to 4.5 years following treatment. These findings provided support for the long-term effects of such an approach in changing noncompliant and deviant behaviors.

The approach employed at the University of Georgia differs from the work of the OSLC in several major ways. In Georgia, for example, the involvement of both parents in the treatment program is not mandatory, and the children are younger. The essence of both programs, however, involves teaching parents to alter immediate parental antecedents and consequences of deviant and positive child behaviors.

Given the research conducted on parent-training programs, it is not surprising that reviews of treatment programs for aggressive, antisocial children reveal that behavioral parent training is an efficacious method for modifying the behavior of children with oppositional defiant and conduct disorders (Kazdin, 1988; McCauley, 1988; Moreland, Schwebel, Beck, & Wells, 1982). However, inconsistencies in the findings of the follow-up studies and thus the maintenance of treatment effects suggest that further work needs to be conducted to determine the effects of other family and parental variables on treatment outcome and maintenance.

Social Learning Family Therapy

Although parent-training approaches to treating children with oppositional defiant and conduct disorders has been helpful, there have continued to be shortcomings in the form of failure to generalize and to maintain treatment gains, as well as difficulty in engaging family members in the process. Griest and Wells (1983) presented an excellent review of the literature relating to the "state of the art" of family therapy for conduct disorders from a learning perspective. These authors stated that a current understanding of working with aggressive, antisocial, disruptive children must be based on two perspectives. First, great strides have already occurred in our understanding of the etiology and treatment of childhood aggression. Second, wide gaps still exist in our understanding of several familial variables and their relationship to the treatment of antisocial children.

The emphasis of therapy with aggressive-child families has been based on the assumption that a child's behavior is largely determined by situations that occur within the family between the parent(s) and the child. The focus of therapy has then centered on the modification of contingencies and the teaching of parenting skills. For the most part, either other aspects of parent functioning have been ignored, or it has been assumed that once target-child behavior problems are controlled, then these other aspects of parental functioning will become stabilized.

Clinical experience, as well as emerging research findings, has begun to indicate that parent training is not always successful in reducing antisocial behavior, nor are gains always maintained over time (Bernal, Klinnert, & Schultz, 1980; Eyberg & Johnson, 1974; Johnson & Christensen, 1975; Wahler, 1980). In his review of parent-training programs, McCauley (1988) reported a similar finding: that whereas overall parent training seems to be helpful, there are situations where it either does not work or does not maintain. This is particularly true when other correlates of child deviance are evident, as is the case with marital discord, economic crises, and related issues. He suggested that parent-training programs are most successful in families in which the parent–child relationship is the only major family problem.

Griest and Wells (1983) stated that "it is only recently that the treatment vehicle in parent training has been identified as potentially requiring intervention in areas other than child-management skills" (p. 38). For effective treatment of children with antisocial behaviors, within a family context, attention must be paid to additional areas of family functioning for treatment to have the impact necessary for maintaining positive change. Additional components to be addressed include cognitive functioning of the parents, parents' physiological status, marital circumstances and conflict, and social variables.

McMahon and Forehand (1984) observed that family-related issues (viz., parent perception of a child's behavior, parental extrafamilial relationships, parent personal adjustment, and marital satisfaction) are associated with child behavior problems. Consequently, these issues may inhibit the effectiveness of a parent-training model using a behavioral approach. However, these issues are often neglected by clinicians and researchers.

Todd and Stanton (1983) and Olson, Russell, and Sprenkle (1980) have indicated that behavioral family therapy may be regarded as the treatment of choice for children with conduct disorder problems. A family therapy model offers the therapist an opportunity to focus treatment strategies on the compounding variables of parental or familial functioning not otherwise addressed in a more restricted parent-training or child management program. Thus, behavioral family therapy has outgrown the less complex parent-training model and has been made increasingly more comprehensive by the inclusion of numerous family variables in the identification and treatment of antisocial child behaviors. Assessment procedures have been expanded to include parent perceptions of child behaviors and child problem-solving abilities, parent psychological factors (viz., depression), marital issues (viz., marital conflict, satisfaction), and social issues (viz., family environment, extrafamilial relationships, school environment).

Parental Perceptions of the Antisocial Child. Parental perceptions of the antisocial child are important in distinguishing clinical from nonclinical samples of children and for treatment intervention. Lobitz and Johnson (1975) confirmed that children referred to a clinic for treatment demonstrated significantly more disruptive behavior and less prosocial behavior than those in a nonreferred comparison group; mothers of clinic children displayed significantly more negative and commanding behaviors; and, of considerable importance, 90% of clinic children and 90% of nonclinic children could be correctly classified on the basis of the negativism and commanding behavior of the parent. Griest, Forehand, Wells, and McMahon (1980) conducted a similar study and found the mother's personal adjustment was predictive of whether the child was referred for clinical treatment. Many children referred for treatment could not be differentiated from nonclinic children based on their behaviors, but mothers perceived their children to be deviant. Forehand and King (1974) propose that modifying parental perceptions be a goal for therapists treating children with conduct disorders, although Griest and Wells (1983) state that the relationship between parental perceptions and actual child behavior is quite complex. If parents' perceptions of their children's behaviors are not always accurate, it is possible that other variables, such as parental adjustment, enter into the decision to label a child as deviant.

P. W. Morris et al. (1988), in a comparative study of fathers of aggressive boys and fathers of well-behaved boys, examined paternal thoughts during the playback of videotapes of fathers in problem-solving activities with their children. Fathers of aggressive children had more negative attitudes toward their sons and listed more negative and fewer positive thoughts about their children and their families. This study adds more support for the inclusion of treatment interventions that directly address the parental cognitions of aggressive children in any program that provides therapeutic assistance to this population.

Out of the evaluations of parental perceptions of children has come the conclusion that parents do not always accurately perceive their children's behavior before treatment or after termination of treatment. At times, they rate their children as more deviant than the children are observed to be; conversely, at other times the children are not rated as aggressive as they actually are. Wahler and Afton (1980), in studying this phenomena, found that, although all of the families they treated showed positive gains, treatment gains were maintained only by those who displayed perceptual as well as behavioral changes.

Wells (1981) suggested that three groups of children referred to a child outpatient clinic can be identified: (a) behaviorally and/or emotionally deviant children whose parents' perceptions are accurately based on their child's behavior, (b) children who are behaviorally and/or emotionally deviant but whose parents' perceptions are also influenced by their own maladjustment, and (c) relatively normal children whose parents' perceptions are inaccurate and are based on their own personal maladjustment, low tolerance for stress, or high standards of acceptability rather than on the child's actual behavior. Griest and Wells (1983) believe that traditional parent training inadequately services families in the second group by ignoring cognitive variables that contribute to perceived or actual deviance. We agree, but extend that concern to include the third group as well.

Problem-Solving Abilities. A second area of cognitive parent variables that has received limited attention in research on antisocial children is problem-solving abilities and efficiency. Patterson (1982) stated that it is assumed that parents of antisocial, aggressive children are less skilled in solving family problems than are parents of normal children. Patterson (1982) went on to state:

> Families of conduct-problem children have a long history of failure in solving problems. Their efforts to solve crises and conflicts are not followed by perceivable changes in anyone's behavior. Even if a discussion results in some type of an agreement, the changes are either temporary, or simply never occur. (pp. 229–230)

The research findings of Spivack, Platt, and Shure (1976) supported the hypothesis that the aggressive behavior of children and adolescents is in part a function of inadequate interpersonal cognitive problem-solving skills, and, in fact, a relationship between problem-solving ability and behavioral adjustment has been supported for other age groups and populations.

Three specific areas in which delinquent populations show deficits were identified by Little and Kendall (1979): problem solving, role taking, and self-control. They also outlined a set of abilities necessary for successful coping in interpersonal situations, which includes sensitivity to interpersonal problems, a tendency to link cause and effect spontaneously (causal thinking), readiness to view possible consequences of actions (consequential thinking), the ability to generate solutions (alternative thinking), the ability to conceptualize step-by-step means for reaching specific goals (means–end thinking), and the ability to view situations from another person's perspective (perspective taking).

It seems reasonable to posit that children learn their interpersonal cognitive problem-solving skills from parents who model such abilities. Spivack et al. (1976) reported that in fact there is a positive correlation between parental ability to solve problems, children's ability to solve problems, and behavior problems. P. W. Morris et al. (1988) found that fathers of well-behaved boys were more efficient problem solvers and more frequently modeled behavior designed to reach agreeable problem solutions than did fathers of aggressive boys. Likewise, these fathers engaged in significantly more positive solution behaviors and facilitated problem solving by engaging in more constructive, problem-oriented behaviors, resulting in agreements. These findings support the inclusion of cognitive problem-solving training in treatment programs designed to address the problems of families with conduct-disordered children if treatment gains are to be maintained.

Other researchers and clinicians have conducted training in problem-solving and communications skills, but there has been a lack of generalization — the skills may be learned, but they do not always generalize to other settings (Foster, Prinz, & O'Leary, 1983). In fact, good communication skills have been demonstrated by family members before entering therapy. This finding raises the question of whether poor communications and problem-solving ability reflect a skill deficit or a performance deficit. The need to address parental cognitive components in treatment seems apparent, given the questionable effectiveness of parental communication skills and their apparent inefficient problem-solving capabilities.

Parent Psychological Variables

There is a relationship between parents' psychological adjustment and deviant child behaviors. Parents' personal adjustment and marital adjustment influence the behavior of the parents and of the children involved. It has been found that there is a direct relationship between fathers' clinical Minnesota Multiphasic Personality Inventory (MMPI) scales and the deviance level of their aggressive children (Johnson &

Lobitz, 1974). Other reports have found that mothers of conduct problem children experience higher levels of depression and anxiety than mothers of normal children (Griest et al., 1980), and that depression levels of parents can be a significant predictor of dropout during treatment (McMahon et al., 1981).

A number of these issues are of questionable etiology, apparent "chicken-or-egg" dilemmas. Does maternal depression cause conduct-disordered children or does clinical disturbance of fathers, as measured by the MMPI, cause aggressive children? Or does a highly aggressive child cause parents to be depressed or disturbed? There are no clear answers to these questions, but there is a need to address family factors when treating antisocial children. It is likely that the behaviors of spouses and children have a significant impact on parenting, with the result being that parental behavior has a significant impact on the children involved. A treatment program that addresses only one unit of the interactional system will not be as powerful as one that encounters the entire family system. If parental moods are modified during treatment, change is more likely to occur for the whole family and the gains are likely to be maintained at follow-up; if left unaddressed, the depressive state of parents can lead to early withdrawal from treatment.

Marital Variables

Clear evidence exists that children with higher rates of disruptive behavior are more likely to have parents with marital problems than are children with lower rates of disruptive behavior. There is a consistent negative relationship between marital satisfaction and the observance of problem behaviors in children (Johnson & Lobitz, 1974), and there is a relationship between marital satisfaction and parental negativeness toward the child.

At times, treatment of conduct problem children in a family model can result in improvement in marital relationships, although it is doubtful that the changes will maintain unless marital satisfaction becomes a targeted goal of the treatment (Forehand, Wells, McMahon, & Griest, 1982).

Griest and Wells (1983) have stated that when a relationship does exist between marital discord and child behavior problems, clinicians and researchers alike often assume that marital discord causes or exacerbates child behavior problems, rather than vice versa. This assumption is not confirmed by the research, and it may very well be that having a child with a conduct disorder in the family serves as a precursor of marital adjustment problems, or that other psychological processes contribute to the occurrence of both (e.g., lack of problem-solving skills, depression). Therefore, no specific or precise explanation of the relationship between marital discord and child behavior problems can be elucidated; however, further investigation into this relationship is clearly warranted.

Social Variables

Increasing attention is being directed toward the effect of parents' extrafamilial contacts on the occurrence of disruptive childhood behaviors (Szykula, Mas, Turner, Crowley, & Sayger, 1989). In addition, there is evidence that the child's school environment and the general family environment may affect the occurrence of childhood aggression.

Wahler (1980) found that maternal social contacts may affect the interactional pattern within the mother–child relationship. He reported that when mothers had a high number of contacts with friends, their negative actions toward their children decreased, but when they had fewer contacts outside the home, their negative reactions increased. Wahler (1980) referred to mothers with few contacts out of the home as "insular mothers." They are characterized by infrequent and aversive social contacts with relatives or social agencies. In a comparison of treatment effects for insular and noninsular families, Wahler and Afton (1980) found that noninsular mothers improved their interactions with their children and maintained these gains at follow-up. Insular mothers made similar treatment gains, but they did not maintain their positive changes. As a result of the Wahler research, it appears that maternal social contacts outside the home, both in quality and quantity, are related to the mother–child interactional patterns within the home. Maternal insularity must be addressed in effective family intervention programs for conduct-disordered children.

Family Environment

A number of factors within the family environment itself have been examined in the context of their influence on the development and maintenance of aggressive child behavior. Many authors have noted several predisposing factors of conduct disorders that relate to family environment (APA, 1987; Patterson, 1982; Quay, 1986a). Parental rejection, inconsistent management with harsh discipline, frequent shifting of parental figures, large family size, absent father, and parental figures with antisocial personality disorder and alcohol dependence have all been associated with the occurrence of aggressive children in families. Further, conduct disorders are overly represented at the lower socioeconomic levels and where less maternal and overly restrictive and rigid paternal disciplinary patterns are present (Goldman, Stein, & Guerry, 1983; Martin, 1988).

Within the social learning theoretical framework, it seems appropriate to discuss the family environment as one within which various modes of aggressive behavior are learned through models. Observing other individuals behave aggressively without noticeable adverse consequences tends to increase the likelihood that the observer will engage in aggressive, antisocial behaviors. Subsequently, as the aversive behaviors increase in frequency with one family member, the aversive response behaviors on the part of another family member are likely to increase. The identification of this negatively reinforcing interactional pattern has led Patterson (1982) to hypothesize about the coercive family process in aggressive-child families. This process is characterized by high rates of conflict and the subsequent placement of parents in a position to deal with more aversive events than in families of nondeviant children.

This prediction has been born out by P. W. Morris et al. (1988), who found that fathers of aggressive boys perceived their family members as less concerned, supportive, and open than did fathers of well-behaved boys. Also, fathers of well-behaved boys perceived their families as more cohesive, more expressive, and less conflictual than did fathers of aggressive boys, whereas fathers of aggressive boys demonstrated more negative and fewer positive thoughts about their families. These findings led the present authors to speculate that a child subjected to more frequent critical evaluations by family members could develop a poorer self-image, resulting in a predisposition toward acting more aggressively, particularly in threatening interpersonal situations.

Marital status may influence the home environment. Examining aggressive behavior in normal and deviant members of intact versus mother-only families yielded interesting results (Horne, 1981). Clinic-referred families, as expected, demonstrated higher rates of aggressive behaviors than did normal families. Further, within the clinic-referred group, mother-only families had higher rates of aggressive behavior than did intact families, whereas mother-only normal families had lower rates of aggression than intact, clinic-referred families. Fathers may be a stabilizing factor for deviant families, but in families without an antisocial child, this stabilizing factor may not be necessary. Having controlled for the variables of socioeconomic level, number of children, and age, Horne (1981) concluded that factors other than the presence or absence of a father appear to have a greater importance in determining the frequency of aggressive behavior by family members. These findings are consistent with Patterson et al. (1975) who indicated that if there is an identified aggressive target child, all family members are likely to emit a high rate of aggressive behavior, regardless of the number of parents or the socioeconomic status.

Research on family variables suggests most strongly that treatment of oppositional-defiant- and conduct-disordered children should include, in the gamut of concerns addressed, such stressors as being a single parent, discipline methods, aggressive behaviors of siblings and parents, family conflict and expressiveness, and family relationships needing modification during the treatment program. These variables need to be directly addressed or modified during the treatment phase so that family members may learn the skills necessary to manage their lives, including their antisocial children, in a more productive and meaningful manner.

School Environment and Peer Relations

Behavioral treatment programs have been criticized for ignoring the way in which families and school environments encourage deviance (Blechman, 1985). Cole, Dodge, and Coppotelli (1982) reported that peer rejection, as a criterion measure, can be used to differentiate between children who are actively disliked (i.e., aggressive) and those who are neglected (i.e., withdrawn) by their peers. Aggressive, argumentative, and disruptive behaviors characterize rejected children. Patterson (1982) concluded that the covariation between poor peer relations and delinquent behavior is so reliable that it is now a regular feature in longitudinal studies designed to predict later delinquency.

There appears to be a strong relationship between behaviors learned in the family environment and behaviors exhibited at school, although it is not a direct one-to-one relationship. Patterson and Reid (1984) have noted that most family-based approaches have not extended the generalization of the socialization process beyond the home environment, although that is clearly the direction that family treatment of antisocial children should take.

Related to the need to address school issues through a family context, Forehand, Long, Brody, and Fauber (1985) examined home behavior patterns to predict achievement and social behavior of children in the school setting. They found that the most significant predictor of externalizing, acting-out behavior problems was the child's relationship with the mother, whereas the relationship with the father was the best predictor of school grades. All measures of the child's school performance (viz., school grades, teacher-completed assessment of internalizing problems, teacher assessment of externalizing problems) were related to maternal depression. In terms of long-term considerations, not only should the mother–child relationship be examined in relation to cross-setting influences in school, but the mother's personal adjustment and the father's relationship with the child should also be addressed. This recommendation is consistent with the Horne and Van Dyck (1983) study on baseline variables as predictors of successful treatment, which found that the rates of aggressive behavior and child school problems were highly predictive of successful treatment outcomes.

When implementing treatment approaches for reducing oppositional defiant or conduct disorder behaviors, it is appropriate that peer relationships and the school setting be important factors included in the therapy process.

Overview of a Treatment Program

Based on the findings presented above, a treatment program addressing the needs of oppositional-defiant- and conduct-disordered children will be most effective when the following components are included:

1. Assessment that clearly defines problem areas and establishes goals for treatment consistent with the problems being encountered by the family
2. Involvement of the multiple systems involved, including parents, siblings, school personnel, and others
3. Effective therapeutic intervention skills which include impacting the environment and establishing positive expectations for change
4. Developing self-control skills for the entire family such that parents and children have alternatives to explosive or depressive behavior
5. Defining disciplinary approaches that lead to positive changes for all family members
6. Social enhancement methods for increasing prosocial behaviors of children
7. Programs for intervening in other systems, including the extended family, school, and community agencies
8. Maintenance skills for continuing change once it has occurred.

The following chapters describe a treatment approach that has been successfully used to address the problems of antisocial children through a family intervention model (Fleischman & Horne, 1979; Sayger, Horne, Passmore, & Walker, 1988).

Chapter 4
Child and Family Assessment

The decision about which assessment procedures should be used is determined by the reason for collecting the information. When working with oppositional-defiant- and conduct-disordered children using a multidimensional approach, as is appropriate based on the review of literature related to treatment programs described in earlier chapters, a broad scope of assessment is necessary. A great quantity of assessment tools is available for therapists, and the selection will be based on availability of materials, resources for scoring and evaluating the measures, and the likelihood of using the information gleaned from the assessment devices.

Excellent resources exist for developing assessment programs for children who are oppositional-defiant- and conduct-disordered. Ollendick and Hersen (1984), for example, have provided an edited text which outlines principles and procedures for behavioral assessment programs, including specific assessment strategies (e.g., behavioral interviewing, behavioral checklists and rating scales, self-report instruments, peer sociometric forms, self-monitoring procedures, direct observation, intellectual and academic achievement tests). Martin (1988) has provided a broader presentation of personality assessment for children with behavior problems. In this chapter we describe the assessment process we use in our treatment program.

FAMILY INFORMATION

The treatment focus of this book is antisocial children. We have established that children's behavior is functional within a social context. The social context in which conduct- and/or oppositional-defiant-disordered children learn to interact in antisocial ways is in the family, and that is the place where we begin our assessment.

Demographic Information

We begin with a family demographic orientation in order to develop a picture of the family and to better understand the interrelationships within and among the various family members.

The Family Intake Form was developed to obtain information mostly concerning the child identified by the family, school, courts, or other referral source as the oppositional-defiant- or conduct-disordered child. The form provides information about the reason for the referral, the referral source, what prescription drugs the child is taking, and any identified handicaps or disabilities. Further information is gathered regarding the parental reports of problems at home and school and the length of time problems have existed. There also are items designed to determine whether the behavior meets the oppositional defiant or conduct disorder criteria of the DSM-III-R.

Information about family members is also obtained in Part A of the intake form. The form lists queries about socioeconomic items (viz., education, occupation, income), other persons residing in the home, and additional problems or concerns the family may be experiencing. Part B of the intake form provides information in a summary form indicating relationships, ages, and other relevant demographic information. We also use a second copy of Part B as part of our termination report. Information is gathered to determine whether changes have occurred in any of the items since therapy began.

An assessment instrument we call the Factors Contributing to Change Scale (FCCS) (see Appendix A) (Horne & Sayger, 1989a) has been developed to assist us in gathering information about the probability of success with the family based on environmental and family conditions. The scale is still in the developmental stages, although we have predictive data on approximately 50 families and we are currently analyzing the data to determine the effectiveness of the scale in predicting the outcome of intervention procedures. The FCCS provides information about access to transportation and telephones, stability of schedules, parental support, and other related items. The form is completed by the therapist as fully as possible, and then missing items of information are gathered during a subsequent meeting with the family. An alternate form, the Post-Factors Contributing to Change scale, is used to assess factors identified as contributing to change.

A Therapist Termination Report (Horne, 1989) is completed by the therapist at the end of treatment and identifies areas addressed during treatment, success of the family in applying specific procedures, and the likelihood of treatment maintenance. This report has been particularly useful for examining changes in the family and identifying which families are likely to sustain the changes they have made during treatment. This form is also helpful to agencies treating families who are likely to be returning for additional help as time passes — a common situation for families with oppositional-defiant- and conduct-disordered children.

A Parents Rating Form (PRF) (Horne & Sayger, 1989b) — adapted from the work of Sayger and Szykula (1987) and Szykula, Sayger, Morris, and Sudweeks (1987) — is completed by the parents after treatment is concluded. An alternative to having the parents complete the form is for a member of the agency to meet with the family as an uninvolved third party (e.g., a quality control representative from the agency), particularly for families that have difficulty reading and writing. The PRF accesses additional information from the parents regarding the positive and negative experiences of their participation in the treatment. Parents are asked to list the positive and negative effects of the treatment on their family members in seven areas, including themselves, their spouse, other children in the family, and the identified child. Copies of the Post-Factors Contributing To Change, Therapist Termination Reports, and Parents Rating Form are available, on request, from the authors.

Family Environment Scale

The FES (Moos, 1974; Moos & Moos, 1984) was developed to provide information about the climate of the family. Three domains of family functioning have been identified which encompass 10 subscales.

1. The Relationship Domain, is measured by the Cohesion, Expressiveness, and Conflict subscales. The subscales address the manner in which family members interact, including how expressive they are in their feelings, amount of conflict which exists within the family structure, and the extent of their cohesiveness.
2. The Personal Growth Domain, or goal orientation, is measured by the Independence, Achievement Orientation, Intellectual-Cultural-Orientation, Active-Recreational Orientation, and Moral-Religious Emphasis subscales. The Personal Growth Domain identifies the extent to which the family promotes personal growth of its individual members, including allowing family members to make their own decisions, act autonomously, and individuate from other family members. Further, it addresses the extent of family members' participation and involvement in social and cultural activities, and examines religious and ethical issues of the family.
3. The System Maintenance Domain is measured by the Organization and Control subscales. It identifies family organization and structure,

and is useful for understanding the degree to which family members adhere to a family rule system.

While the specific behavioral components of family interactions are important, the broader concepts measured by the FES provide valuable information for comparing families coming for treatment with normative groups identified by Moos. We use the FES as a before-and-after instrument to determine changes that occur as a result of treatment.

Family Problem-Solving Interaction

As a part of the initial interview, family members are asked to interact in problem-solving activities. We have developed a Common Problem Checklist (see Appendix B) from which parents and children select a concern for the problem-solving discussion. These family discussions of the selected problems are videotaped for coding purposes. The problem-solving activities are then scored using the Family Problem-Solving Behavior Coding System (Nickerson, Light, Blechman, & Gandelman, 1976, Winter), as revised by Fuelle (1981). Trained raters view and code each interaction that occurs during the videotaped problem-solving discussion. Interactions are classified according to 28 verbal and nonverbal codes.

A second part of the Family Problem-Solving Behavior Coding System is the Problem-Solving Efficiency Scale, also by Nickerson et al. (1976, Winter). This scale is intended to measure how well family members work together toward solving a problem. The total score achieved by the family represents the extent to which they can solve the problem being discussed, with the range being from a high of 4 (where the dyad reaches a solution that is agreeable to all involved) to a low of 1 (where at least one member of the dyad does not talk about the problem).

Beavers–Timberlawn Family Evaluation Scale

The BTFES (Lewis, Beavers, Gossett, & Phillips, 1976) was developed to assess the interactional patterns characteristic of healthy functioning families. To examine these patterns, the same videotape developed for use with the Family Problem-Solving Behavior Coding System and the Problem-Solving Efficiency Scale is rated by trained observers. This scale consists of 13 single-item scales subsumed under five theoretical domains, including Family Structure (Overt Power, Parental Coalitions, Closeness), Autonomy (Self-disclosure, Responsibility, Invasiveness, Permeability), Affect (Expressiveness, Mood and Tone, Conflict, Empathy), Perception of Reality (Family Mythology), and Task Efficiency (Goal-Directed Negotiation). Each of these scales is rated on a 1 to 5 Likert scale. Although the authors admit to numerous areas of scale overlap, each scale is believed to express an essential construct used in assessing family system functioning. The authors of the scale indicate that it is useful for differentiating among four groups: healthy families and families containing a neurotic, behavior-disordered, or psychotic adolescent.

Child Behavior Checklist

The CBCL (Achenbach & Edelbrock, 1983) contains 118 behavior problem items plus items for reporting a child's school performance and the amount and quality of his or her participation in sports, games, hobbies, chores, organizations, and social relationships. Parents complete this form, evaluating their child's behavior before and after treatment in our program. The scales of particular relevance to the treatment of antisocial children are: Depressed, Hyperactive, Aggressive, Delinquent, Internalizing, Externalizing, Sum T, and Social Competence.

Parent Daily Report

The PDR (Patterson, Reid, Jones, & Conger, 1975) records the occurrence or nonoccurrence of specified problem behaviors. Parents record data at the end of each day for three consecutive days at pretreatment and then maintain their recording of behaviors during treatment. Patterson et al. (1975) have indicated that asking parents to make a decision about whether a behavior occurred or did not occur covering only the preceding 8 to 10 hours minimizes distortions in memory and judgment.

The first 19 items are used to rate positive behaviors, with parents putting a check mark beside behaviors that did occur and leaving the others blank. Examples include: Complies to all requests; Does homework without prodding; Accepts disappointment well; Shows happiness, smiles a lot, laughs; Shows affection, hugs, kisses; Gets chores done on time.

The next 19 items are negative behaviors, and the parents similarly check any negative items that occurred throughout a given day of monitoring. Examples are: Argues, talks back to parent(s)/other adults; Cries or whines; Noncompliant, defiant; Abuses animals; Bedwets, wets pants, soils; Hits, kicks, bites others.

It is possible to derive both a positive behavior and a negative behavior score. Patterson, Reid, and Maerov (1978) reported that PDR scores at termination function as the best predictor of status at follow-up. The termination PDR score was in 83% agreement with follow-up PDR scores and in 58% agreement with Total Deviant Behavior follow-up scores.

Dyadic Adjustment Scale

The DAS (Spanier, 1979; Spanier & Thompson, 1982) was designed to assess quality of marriage or similar dyads. The DAS is a 32-item self-report measure which may be used as part of a clinical interview to examine four factor patterns of the couple's relationship. The four factors are:

1. Affectional expression
2. Dyadic satisfaction
3. Dyadic cohesion
4. Dyadic consensus.

Spanier (1979) stated that the DAS can be used best in one of three ways:

> First, as a very general indicator, to help formulate an overall impression of the quality of the marital relationship; second, a husband's and wife's responses can be compared, and the similarities and differences used as a starting point for discussions; third, specific problem areas can be identified by examination of responses to individual items or to the subscales, and these responses can serve as a basis for discussion and for the development of a treatment program. (p. 298)

With a theoretical scale range from 0 to 151, the DAS offers researchers and clinicians a brief and highly reliable (Spanier & Thompson, 1982) assessment of marital relationships with the opportunity to focus directly on any of the four factor patterns without losing confidence in the scale's reliability and validity.

Locke–Wallace Marital Adjustment Test

The LWMAT (Locke & Wallace, 1959) has been used extensively as a self-report measure of general marital satisfaction. Each marital partner rates overall marital satisfaction on a 7-point scale, and then the extent of accordance with his or her spouse on eight areas of marital relationship is examined. These areas are:

• Handling family finances
• Matters of recreation
• Demonstration of affection
• Friends

- Sex relationships
- Conventionality
- Philosophy of life
- Ways of dealing with in-laws.

Marital adjustment is of particular interest when working with families with oppositional-defiant- or conduct-disordered children. There is support in the family therapy systems literature for the position that disruptive, antisocial children may represent a dysfunctional family system. Others have taken the position even further, indicating that such children behave as they do as a way of getting parents with a dysfunctional marital relationship in for help — the object of treatment is the marital relationship, not the dysfunctional child.

Our experience in working with families with antisocial children is that approximately 50% of them are experiencing marital conflict in conjunction with having a disruptive child. However, this also means that half of the families are not experiencing marital conflict. For the families that are not experiencing marital difficulties, treatment focuses on the child within the family system. For the families that are experiencing marital problems, the issues are dealt with directly, early in treatment, to determine whether the conflict is indeed the area that must be addressed. We have found that marital counseling in families that report considerable marital conflict may result in effective changes on the part of the children without making them the major focus of treatment. This situation, however, occurs in a minority of cases. The majority need attention to the child or the child and the marital relationship. Even in cases where marital conflict has been reported by parents, often the conflict exists because there is so much turmoil over the child's behavior in the family, and the marital relationship improves significantly when the child's behavior improves.

Beck Depression Inventory

The BDI (Beck, 1967, 1972) is a 21-item self-report measure which gives a rapid assessment of the severity of depression as well as specific symptoms. In addition, the various items on the BDI provide information regarding the individual's central concerns.

The BDI is used to determine the extent to which one or both parents are experiencing depression, a condition that may be debilitating. One aspect of treatment is to have parents establish responsible power in the family, but the establishment of power will not occur if one or both parents are too depressed to follow through on treatment recommendations.

Symptom Checklist 90-R

The SCL-90-R (Derogatis, 1983) is a 90-item self-report inventory designed to reflect psychological symptom patterns of psychiatric and medical patients. Using a 5-point scale of distress, ranging from 0 = not at all to 5 = extremely, the SCL-90-R provides information on nine primary symptom dimensions:

1. Somatization
2. Obsessive-compulsive
3. Interpersonal sensitivity
4. Depression
5. Anxiety
6. Hostility
7. Phobic anxiety
8. Paranoid ideation
9. Psychoticism.

To provide a more flexible and comprehensive assessment of the client's psychological status, three indexes of distress are also provided through interpretation and scoring of the SCL-90-R (viz., Global Severity Index, Positive Symptom Distress Index, Positive Symptom Total).

Clinicians and researchers may wish to use the SCL-90-R as an assessment of the general psychological status of the parents of conduct- and oppositional-defiant-disordered children. As noted in previous chapters, the incidence of psychological disturbance in parents may be a contributing factor to behavioral disorders in children. Additionally, treatment success will be severely compromised if apparent psychological concerns of the parent are not addressed during the therapeutic intervention.

INFORMATION FROM
THE CHILD

Few instruments have been developed to obtain a "child's-eye view" of child behavior problems and family relationships. The development of such measures is long overdue; however, we have found the following instruments offer some hope for assessment in this area. Readers should be aware that most of these instruments are still in the developmental stage and will require further research for validation and standardization.

Youth Self-Report Form

The YSR (Achenbach & Edelbrock, 1987) was developed to complement the Child Behavior Checklist (CBCL), providing for information from the child to supplement parental observations. It is completed by youths who are 11 to 18 years old and so does not apply to all of the oppositional-defiant- and conduct-disordered children seen for treatment. For ages 11 through 16 the CBCL, YSR, and Teacher Report Form (TRF) (discussed under school assessment), the instrument standardization makes it possible to compare the degree of deviance from normative samples as indicated by the parent, the youth, and the teacher.

The YSR provides information on competence and problem scales. The problem scales are:

1. Depressed
2. Unpopular
3. Somatic Complaints
4. Self-Destructive or Identity Problems
5. Thought Disorder
6. Delinquent
7. Aggressive
8. Other Problems.

The YSR is helpful for providing information about how the youth perceives himself or herself. The information derived is particularly useful when conducting a clinical interview to determine how the child perceives the problems in his or her life.

Semistructured Clinical Interview for Children

The SCIC (Achenbach & McConaughy, 1989) has been developed for use with children aged 6 to 11 and in conjunction with the CBCL and TRF to provide a multiperspective assessment of the child's functioning. The SCIC, according to Achenbach and McConaughy (1989), "assesses the child's thoughts, feelings, and behavior through open-ended questions, probes, and structured tasks" (p. 1). It is recommended that the clinician have the following items available during the child's assessment interview:

1. SCIC Protocol Form

2. SCIC Observation and Self-Report Forms
3. Provisional SCIC Profile for Ages 6 to 11
4. Drawing pad and pencil
5. Peabody Individual Achievement Test (PIAT) or PIAT-R Mathematics and Reading Recognition subtests
6. Soft ball (e.g., Nerf® ball)
7. Play materials
8. Audiotape recorder.

The SCIC Protocol Form assesses seven broad areas of child functioning, including

1. Activities, school, and friends
2. Family relations
3. Fantasies
4. Self-perception and feelings
5. Parent-reported problems
6. Cognitive tasks
7. Screen for fine and gross motor abnormalities.

The SCIC Observation and Self-Report Forms were constructed, according to Achenbach and McConaughy (1989), from CBCL and TRF items considered appropriate for a clinical interview, plus additional items derived especially for the SCIC. The SCIC Observation and Self-Report Forms consist of 226 behaviors rated on a 0 to 3 scale (0 = behavior not observed to 3 = definite occurrence of behavior with severe intensity or greater than 3 minutes' duration). These forms provide data across several broad behavioral categories including Inept, Unpopular, Anxious, Withdrawn-Depressed, Inattentive-Hyperactive, Resistant, Family Problems, and Aggressive.

It should be noted that the SCIC is still in the development and standardization phase; however, it appears to be a potentially valuable assessment tool for working with conduct- and/or oppositional-defiant-disordered children.

Children's Version of the Family Environment Scale

The CVFES (Pino, Simons, & Slawinowski, 1984), designed for children between the ages of 5 and 12, is a pictorial, multiple-choice instrument. Using four caricatures representing a father, mother, daughter, and son, the CVFES utilizes the same subscales and family environment domains outlined by the FES (Moos & Moos, 1984). By instructing the child to select the picture that "seems most like your family," the therapist obtains the child's perspective of life in his or her family. The CVFES, as well as the FES, can be employed to obtain information regarding both the perceived and ideal family environments, thus providing an assessment of family satisfaction (Pino, Simons, & Slawinowski, 1983). Although further standardization of the CVFES needs to be completed, it has the potential to be a useful instrument in gaining a more complete view of family relationships and environments for families with acting-out children.

Children's Depression Inventory

The CDI (Kovacs, 1981) is a 27-item inventory which allows a child to select among alternatives on a 3-point scale that reflects the absence, presence, and frequency of occurrence of particular depressive symptoms (0 = symptom is absent to 2 = symptom is severe and present all the time). Providing a range of scores from 0 to 54, the CDI can be administered to children from the ages of 7 to 17 and provides cutoff levels for varying degrees of severity of depression. In a validation study of the CDI, Carlson and Cantwell (1980) found that the instrument was discriminative of children who had been diagnosed as affective-disordered.

Goldman, Stein, and Guerry (1983) state that the CDI provides clinicians and researchers assessing childhood depression with certain advantages in that it is simple to score and has undergone extensive field testing. These authors also identify two areas of possible concern. First, they question whether children have the ability to report their own symptoms because many children avoid expressing depressed affect. Second, Goldman et al. point out that children function at differing levels of cognitive and language skills; thus, the answers they provide to such a self-report inventory may be open to varying interpretations.

Some children with conduct or oppositional defiant disorders may also display behaviors consistent with depression symptomatology. Clinicians working with this population may choose the CDI as a brief assessment of the child's current depressive symptoms.

SCHOOL INFORMATION

There are a variety of types of information that may be obtained from school personnel. We generally request the information described in the following sections, but additional types of data are available, depending on the type of information needed for treatment, the cooperation of school personnel, and the resources of the treatment agency. Types of information that might be of interest include sociometric measures, such as peer evaluations, and behavioral observations obtained by trained raters.

Teacher Interview

Our experience in working with teachers has been very positive. Whereas many professionals have reported that teachers do not seem to place student needs high on their priority lists, we have not experienced this situation. What we have experienced is that a number of teachers are exasperated and taxed by very difficult children and do not know what to do to help them. When they learn that there is a chance of getting help for the child (which can result in a more pleasant classroom atmosphere for both students and teacher), teachers can be most helpful and beneficial in the treatment program.

Academic Performance

Most antisocial children have experienced little academic success in school. There often is an extensive academic file available from school personnel, particularly from school psychologists who have evaluated the student to determine the nature of the problems he or she has experienced. Many of the referrals we receive are from school psychologists who have evaluated children and determined that, although they may not be performing well academically, treatment needs to focus on behavioral and emotional problems which may be beyond the ability of school personnel to provide.

Academic records contain information about standardized assessment of academic achievement (e.g., achievement tests, such as the Iowa Test of Basic Skills), grades earned, teacher observations, and special testing evaluations performed. Information about such topics as learning disabilities, intellectual impairment, and measures of developmental problems are frequently available from school files.

Daily Behavior Checklist

The DBC (Prinz, Conner, & Wilson, 1981) is used to sample classroom behavior. Teachers observe and record the child's classroom behavior for five consecutive days. The DBC contains 22 specific behavioral items worded in such a way that the teacher can easily decide whether or not a child performed a specified behavior during the day. A total deviant behavior score is created by summing across the 5 days that teachers observe the behaviors. Sample items include:

- Was out of seat during work time on three or more occasions
- Spoke out of turn on at least one occasion
- Tried to get your attention while you were busy with another child
- Ran around room during work or quiet time.

Teacher Report Form

The Child Behavior Profile of the TRF (Achenbach & Edelbrock, 1986) was developed for completion by teachers to obtain a description of the pupil's behavior as the teacher views it. The TRF, modeled after the CBCL, requests relevant background information, measurements of academic performance, and ratings of adaptive functioning, as well as teacher evaluations of specific problems, as defined by the 118 behavior problems listed.

The profile of the TRF provides normative information on the child's adaptive functioning, including School Performance, Working Hard, Behaving Appropriately, Learning, and Happy. The profile also has the following subscales for problem behaviors:

- Anxious
- Social Withdrawal
- Unpopular
- Self-destructive
- Obsessive-Compulsive
- Inattentive
- Nervous-Overactive
- Aggressive
- Other Problems.

The TRF is particularly useful for incorporating teachers' evaluations, standardized so that comparisons may be made to norm groups, into a more comprehensive evaluation package for understanding the behavioral and emotional patterns of children being referred for treatment.

COMMUNITY AND SOCIAL
SERVICE AGENCY INFORMATION

Within the community setting, oppositional-defiant- and conduct-disordered children often have extensive records which should be incorporated into any treatment program. These records include the following.

Medical Records

Often antisocial children have extensive medical records, at times beginning as early as birth. Medical records frequently document complaints about behavior and personality problems reported by parents early in the child's life. It is particularly useful to have access to medical records because parents sometimes report information that is not reliable. One example is that we often receive parent reports about children who are hyperactive or mentally deficient, whereas school and medical records may not provide any support for the parent's statement. It is important to check out official records rather than accept parent reports. It is also helpful to develop cooperative relationships with the medical community, obtain medical reports, and meet with medical personnel to discuss antisocial problems. This relationship often results in collaborative approaches to addressing the problems of the child.

Court and Police Records

Our experience in working with the antisocial behavior of children is that parents often under- or overreport the extent of police and/or court involvement. With permission from the family, information can be obtained from police and/or court records that may be very beneficial. Information about the number and extent of legal run-ins is helpful in assisting the therapist in defining the depth of the problem. We have found the documentation of theft particularly useful in developing treatment programs. Informal observations made by the staff of juvenile centers or group homes is also very helpful in understanding the youth's reaction to legal encounters: Hostile responses are not as encouraging as responses indicating concern, anxiety, or fear. The collaborative relationship that develops between the treatment program and the legal establishment is very functional for working with antisocial youth.

Child Protective Services Reports

A significant portion of the antisocial youth we work with have been involved with the welfare department of Child Protective Services (CPS) as a result of family abuse and/or neglect. Child Protective Services generally welcomes involvement of a treatment program that offers hope for attending to family interactions that lead to abuse and neglect.

We find that CPS personnel are willing to be involved in many ways, including providing pressure and legal force to have the family participate in counseling relationships. We have received reports of CPS being adversarial toward treatment programs that address the needs of antisocial children, but we have not had that experience at all. CPS staff have been extremely cooperative and helpful, even providing transportation and other support programs for families involved in our treatment program. The important balance therapists must achieve is to work cooperatively with CPS while at the same time remaining objective and independent of the expectations that they may place on a therapeutic program, expectations which may run contrary to professional treatment plans.

Group Home Records

Group homes exist in many communities for the placement of antisocial children. Often they are directed and managed by CPS and represent an extension of welfare department offerings to care for troubled youth and families. Because the staff of group homes work directly on a 24-hour schedule with youth placed in the homes, they can provide a wealth of information about the way the child interacts with other residents and staff. They may provide additional observations that are highly useful in developing a treatment program. Again, we have found staff to be extremely helpful and cooperative when they learn that a therapeutic program is being instituted for a resident.

Chapter 5
Initiating Treatment

ESTABLISHING A THERAPEUTIC CLIMATE

The majority of people referred for treatment for oppositional or conduct disorder behavior problems are defensive and suspicious of the services to which they are referred. The service represents a change agent for the agency making the referral, and patients generally are not involved on their own initiative. Psychologists, counselors, or other mental health practitioners are perceived not as friendly support personnel but as coercive agents of change. Therefore, efforts to create an environment conducive to change are important.

The Setting

It is important to consider the setting for providing services. Our experience has been that clients respond better to an informal office and therapeutic setting than they do to one more formal, particularly if they are low-income or low-educational-level clients. Although some appear to be impressed by more formal office arrangements, formality is one way of distancing the therapist from the client, which may prove to be antitherapeutic.

The Relationship

An extensive literature exists describing the therapeutic skills needed for effective relationship enhancement, and others have addressed skills particularly relevant to working with antisocial children and their families. Alexander, Barton, Schiavo, and Parsons (1976), for example, have described therapist characteristics that contribute to effective change when working with delinquents' families, and Morris, Alexander, and

Waldron (1988) have addressed therapist relationship skills that ease resistance issues when working with families of delinquents.

A more specific delineation of clinical skills utilized by therapists has been presented by Fleischman, Horne, and Arthur (1983). They completed a post-hoc analysis of several hundred hours of therapy tapes from families with antisocial children who were receiving treatment and, using the critical-incident approach described by Flanagan (1954), identified the following essential clinical skills:

Building Relationships
    Communicate empathy
    Provide reassurance and normalize problems
    Use self-disclosure
    Define everyone as a victim
    Emphasize positive expectations for change
    Match your communication style to the family
    Use humor

Gathering Information
    Use open-ended questions
    Paraphrase and summarize
    Gather information about what people do
    Gather information about cognitive/emotional reactions
    Gather information about sequences and patterns

Maintaining Structure
    Share the agenda
    Deal with one issue or task at a time
    Break complex problems into manageable units
    End sidetracking
    Give everyone a chance to participate

Teaching New Skills
    Describe skills in specific, nontechnical language
    Provide rationales
    Model the skill
    Check for comprehension
    Couple negative feedback with positive statements

Insuring Implementation of Skills
    Personalize in-session rehearsals
    Pre-problem-solve potential difficulties
    Solicit and anticipate concerns
    Predict feelings and behavior changes

Promoting Independence and Generalization
    Encourage client initiative
    Reinforce client initiative and give credit for positive changes
    Interpret situations from a social learning perspective

Handling Resistance
    Determine why clients resist

Make sure it is not a comprehension problem
Discuss client concerns
Relate tasks to client goals
Modify tasks and assignments. (pp. 48–49)

The skills defined by (Fleischman et al., 1983) are used to establish relationships with the child and the parents. It is clear from the review presented in Chapters 1 through 4 that working with the entire family is the most effective way of helping antisocial children make behavioral changes. While the initial involvement includes working with the entire family, attention must be paid to specific persons or groupings within the family.

Establishing Relationships With the Child

The age of the child referred for treatment influences the way in which the therapist interacts with him or her, as does the nature of the child's problems. A basic element in working with the child is to demonstrate the therapeutic conditions defined above, including acceptance, empathy, and caring. As a part of developing a relationship with the child, the therapist needs to be able to demonstrate an understanding of the function of the antisocial behavior — that the behavior serves a function or a purpose but does not represent craziness or meanness. Helping the client understand the purpose or function of the behavior leads to a discussion of how the purpose may be reasonable but the means for meeting the purpose not acceptable. A client who runs away may be requesting more distancing in the family, which may be a reasonable developmental request, but the therapist must be able to help the client find more adaptable ways of achieving that request, perhaps with school or organized group functions.

In negotiating with the client, the therapist must be able to offer some benefit, for if there is only cost and no advantage, change will not occur. The benefit may take the form of enhanced functioning within the system where the trouble occurs.

1. With the parents:
    Therapist: Melissa, you'd really like to have your mother back off on her yelling, and you'd like your dad to cut out the threats of hitting you. I think that is something we can work on, because, as you know, we work with the whole family and if you're willing to make some changes, I think I can convince your parents to cooperate too.

2. With the school:

> *Therapist:* Jim, the situation is that you don't want to drop out of school but you are so far behind in your academic work that you see no way of hanging in there, and the teacher is constantly hassling you — you seem to feel pretty hopeless, which causes you to strike out at the teacher at times. If I work with you to find better ways of handling the teacher, and to perhaps attend to the school business a little better, would that help you?

3. With courts:

> *Therapist:* So you were doing the shoplifting because you couldn't afford to pay for what you thought you needed. If I work with you to get the judge to back off on the charges, would you work with me to find some other ways of getting what you want, some ways of getting what you need without legal screw-ups?

This early establishment of a therapeutic alliance serves two major functions. First, it demonstrates to the client an understanding (though not an endorsement) of the behavior, which leads to some sense of optimism for possible change. Second, as therapy progresses and stipulations of behavior change are made, the therapist is able to remind the client of the early agreement that they would work together.

> *Therapist:* You know, we have decided to use time-out in your family. Now you say you don't want to go along with time-out, and this is confusing to me. You see, earlier you said you wanted your mom to stop her nagging and constant reminding, and you wanted your dad to stop hitting you or threatening to hit you. Now I'm offering you a way to get what you want, time-out, and you seem reluctant. Help me understand this, do you want your mom to stop her nagging and your dad to stop his hitting? If so, let's give time-out a trial. I know it isn't fun, but it is preferable to nagging and hitting.

The youth must have some sense that change can occur and that the therapist will in fact negotiate with the family or teacher to achieve the goals on which they have agreed.

Establishing a Relationship With the Parents

There are a number of factors that will influence how the parents interact with the therapist. (Note: In this context, "parents" refers to the adults with whom the child resides, whether they are biological parents, stepparents, foster parents, or others.) Foremost is whether the parents are participating voluntarily or involuntarily. If they attend under pressure from the school or the courts, it is much more difficult to enlist their cooperation. When this does occur, though, the situation may be used to develop an alliance with them.

Therapist: I understand the anger you have about being forced to come in for counseling. I wouldn't like to be told I had to do this either. You've talked about the efforts you've used to get Linda to cooperate, to mind, but they don't seem to have worked, so the school has threatened to remove her from school if you don't come for counseling. I'll tell you what I can do. If you are willing to work with me in the program we've got for helping children make some changes, then I'll be glad to work with the school to see if they'll back off a little, to get off your backs, so we can move ahead and get Linda some help. No guarantees, of course, because the school has to do what it has to do, but I've had good luck in the past in getting schools to leave parents and their kids alone while we work on the problems. Would you like to work with me and have me see what I can do with the school?

A very difficult aspect of working with families with aggressive children is making the parents understand and accept that they need to be involved in the treatment program. Usually they respond to the idea of being involved in the program with surprise or at least a lack of enthusiasm, making comments such as, "He's the one with the problem, why do I have to come in? All I want you to do is straighten him out so I don't have to put up with his antics." It is necessary to explain reasons for having the family involved.

Therapist: I understand that you'd like us to work with Kevin and get him straightened up, and we intend to do that. One way we work is to involve the whole family — for a number of reasons. We have some ideas on how to get him to behave better, but we'll be with him only an hour a week; you are with him several hours a day and can see when and how he misbehaves. We can't be at your home to make the observations, so we must rely on you to do that for us. Also, we are pretty certain he misbehaves for a reason — you will be able to see what he does and can help us understand what the reasons are when we meet weekly. Too, we've seen that our work has a good impact on the other kids in the family, and although you haven't complained much about how Sharon and Chuck are doing, if there are any problems there, we can generalize to them too. That would save a lot of time and energy for you on down the road. Finally, you've said you would like some help getting the school out of your business, and when the whole family works together, we move quicker, which can get you free from the school hassles sooner.

Normalizing Problems

Within the family context the problems of the child often are seen as sick, pathological, or in some other sense very abnormal. In counseling it is important to put them in perspective for the family. The approach in working with the family is to confirm that, indeed, the situation is not good, that it is not a happy way to live, but that the problems the family is encountering represent a learning deficit. All families have problems, and all families have difficulty rearing children, but a lot of families are able to figure out ways to handle the problems more effectively. The goal we will develop with the family is to help it understand that the behavior represents purposive, functional behavior operating within a family context, and that it can be changed within that family context.

The question most asked by parents about their child's behavior is, Why does he do these things? The answer we give is: "Why shouldn't he do these things? It is normal for him to do them because he's learned there is a payoff for what he does. When he has a temper tantrum in the grocery store, he gets some candy. When he pushes on the playground, he gets a lot of attention. When he fights other kids, he is able to bully them around. He behaves the way he does because there is a payoff for him, and until there ceases to be a payoff, he will continue to do these things. But that's normal. What you are indicating is that you have a normal child who does some things you don't like, one who gets in trouble. That's what we work on, helping parents figure out how to keep their normal kids from getting into serious abnormal trouble."

During this phase of working with families, the therapist needs to gather information about the function the behavior may serve within the family. Is the child antisocial because of parental deficits (lack of knowledge of how to set limits, poor parenting skills), parental excesses (unpredictable behavior related to excessive drinking, abusive interactions), or other reasons? Through a marriage inventory (e.g., the Locke–Wallace Marital Adjustment Test [LWMAT] or the Dyadic Adjustment Scale [DAS]), the therapist may begin to see that the child's behavior is a way of getting parents to come in for help they are unable to seek themselves. In the family therapy literature there is support for the idea that antisocial children function to get help for parents who are disturbed. We have found in a number of cases that there is a dysfunctional marital dyad, but we don't know whether the child is disruptive because of the dysfunctional marital dyad or whether the marital dyad is dysfunctional because of the acting-out child. We do know that if couples report conflict before treatment begins for the antisocial child, attention must be paid to the marital relationship to see whether it should be the focus of treatment or at least a component of the therapy. It is normal for a child to act in undesirable ways if there is severe conflict between the parents.

Defining All in the Family as Victims

There is usually an identified patient when referrals are made for treatment, the antisocial child, and there is usually an identified victim, frequently the mother. In therapy, all members of the family need to be defined as victims, for, in fact, the family interactions place everyone in the household in a victim role — they all are pained and suffer as a result of the oppositional or conduct disorder in operation:

Therapist: You have been describing what goes on in the family and it sounds as though Amy can be a real hell raiser, and when this happens, Mom, it sounds as though you get very upset and cry a lot. When Mom cries, Dad, it seems you get really angry and start tearing into Amy, which helps slow her down some but results in Mom being upset even more because you got so upset. And the other two kids seem to cower and get frightened when you are riled. Amy gets pained, also, when you spank her or at least send her to her room. The way the situation has been described, I see that Mom is a victim of Amy's aggression, but I also see everyone in the family being a victim of what happens, all of you are pained about what happens. It sounds as though everyone is a victim in aggressive, acting-out situations. One way to stop being a victim is to put a stop to what's going on. That is something we help people with, putting a stop to coercive behavior.

ESTABLISHING POSITIVE EXPECTATIONS FOR CHANGE

Often all members of the family are very discouraged, particularly when they are forced into a treatment program. Although there is no guarantee of success in treatment, there is room for cautious optimism, and that optimism needs to be shared with the parents to help them develop a positive expectation of change.

Therapist: We have worked with a large number of parents and their children, and although we haven't had a perfect success rate, we've found a lot of parents were able to help make some impressive changes in their children's behavior — how they all worked together. That is an advantage of how we work — we are able to assist the whole family in working together to develop the kind of family life-style they want to have.

This approach is based on two considerations: (a) previous experience working with families with acting-out children, and (b) an understanding of the purposiveness of the behavior in question. By helping parents see the functionality of the behavior, it is possible to assist them in determining more effective ways of interacting. This leads to positive expectations for change.

Presenting the Program or Sharing the Agenda

One component of developing a therapeutic climate for the family includes clearly and directly presenting the therapy program. The work we do is quite intensive and requires a commitment from the family to achieve success. Explaining the various components to be covered, the time line anticipated, and the expenses in terms of money and/or energy from the family helps set the stage for cooperation and joining with the family. The information available from the Factors Contributing to Change Scale (FCCS) (Appendix A) is helpful in identifying particular points to attend to when presenting the program to the family, as it provides information that will indicate potential problems in complying with the program. For example, an item such as "Parental time available with the child per day" provides the therapist with some understanding of whether parents will be accessible enough to follow through with assignments.

Sharing the agenda with the family serves an important function, for it provides them with an expectation of what is to be covered in a given session, thereby setting the stage to be task-oriented toward the issues defined. Providing the family with information about what will be covered also allows the therapist to short-circuit sidetracking:

> *Client:* We were using time-out at my mother's house and she told me to stop treating him that way and I told her to mind her own business and she and I started arguing. It was just like the old times, just arguing and fighting. When I was a teen-ager. . . .
> *Therapist:* Excuse me, but let me put us back on talking about time-out. It apparently didn't work well at your mother's, but how has it worked otherwise?

This attention to remaining on task does not imply that genuine concerns people have should be ignored. Rather, as a function of sharing the agenda, the therapist needs to direct the session and only go toward other issues if that is an agreed-on function of the treatment:

> *Therapist:* You have indicated that time-out worked except when you were at your family's house. Is the relationship with your family something we need to talk about, to see how it affects you and your whole family? This way the shift is deliberate and agreed on, not a sidetrack taken.

All Family Members Can Benefit

It is important to point out that a function of using a family treatment approach is that all family members may benefit from participation. The research cited by Patterson (1982) indicates that all members of aggressive, coercive families are victims and experience pain in the interactional process of family life. When all family members have a positive expectation of change, a likelihood of reducing the pain, they are more likely to complete the assignments and activities presented in therapy. Family members who do not see some possibility of a payoff for themselves are not likely to follow through in applying the treatment procedures.

Discuss Previous Success With the Approach

We cannot guarantee successful changes for any individual family. We have worked with enough families, though, to have some idea of the likelihood of change occurring. Using research data (Fleischman & Horne, 1979; Horne & Van Dyck, 1983; Patterson, Reid, Jones, & Conger, 1975; Sayger, Horne, Passmore, & Walker, 1988), it is possible to report that approximately two thirds to three fourths of the children treated in a family program designed to impact antisocial children benefit from the treatment. Behavior change has occurred for others and, given family involvement and follow through, as well as school and community participation, it is possible for the family to effect change with both the targeted child and the rest of the family. The higher the rate of aggressiveness, though, the lower the probability of change (Horne & Van Dyck, 1983; Patterson, 1982), so the family must be cautioned about the requirements of time and energy necessary for the program to be effective.

Discuss Negative Consequences of Not Changing

One aspect of antisocial children is that they seldom get better without intervention in some form (Patterson, 1982). Often families fail to recognize the extent of the problems their children are experiencing and do not identify their children's behavior as dysfunctional. Many assume children will outgrow the behavior, but the "terrible twos" become the "awful adolescents" of a few years later. Wishful thinking is not effective, and parents need to have a clear understanding of how antisocial behavior is likely to escalate, particularly as children approach adolescence and move toward independence and autonomy.

Matching the Family Communication Style

The majority of families with oppositional-defiant- or conduct-disordered children are lower-socioeconomic families, although the range is large. Most therapists are well-educated and quite verbal in their approach. It is important to be aware of and to be able to communicate at the level of the family presenting for therapy. A component of empathy is understanding; families who experience a communication style they perceive as nonaccepting, pompous, affected, or too sophisticated do not feel understood.

The requirement of matching the communication style of the family does not mean therapists have to use the same words, vocabulary, or expressions. Profanity is, at times, used to demonstrate that the therapist "understands," but, in fact, may be seen as pretentious or affected if it is not natural. Matching the family communication style means to be able to explain in terms that are understandable, use expressions with which the family can identify, and personalize the work to the family so it can clearly appreciate that it is the object of attention.

UNDERSTANDING THE PROBLEM

When interviewing the family and attempting to establish a therapeutic environment, it is important to develop a functional analysis of the problem. It is assumed that problems exist within an interactional context comprised of what family members do, what they think, how they feel, and how they interact with others.

What Family Members Do

When family members enter therapy with an antisocial child, they begin by telling what the child does. He or she fights, argues, steals — *does* things. As the therapist listens, she or he attempts to develop an understanding of how the behavior is demonstrated, *what is done.*

What Family Members Think

An adapted form of the model of rational-emotive therapy indicates that

1. A situation occurs.
2. People have thoughts or perceptions about the situation.
3. People feel consistently with how they think.
4. People behave consistently with how they feel.
5. There are consequences for how people behave.

As the therapist listens to the description of what the antisocial child and others in the family do, it is important to understand what each person thinks about the behavior.

> *Therapist:*   Mom, when he yelled at you and stormed out of the room, kicking the screen door and tearing the screen, what were you thinking at that moment?

As has been delineated by Ellis (in press), how people think about a situation has a direct bearing on how they respond to that situation. People who think angry thoughts generally respond in an angry manner. Most families we work with are not attuned to thinking about their thoughts; rather, they assume that situations are independent of their thought processes, or that how they respond is independent of themselves.

> *Mother:* He made me so mad when he kicked that door; I couldn't help myself; I just slapped him as hard as I could when I caught him.

Using therapeutic language that shifts the locus of responsibility from the situation to the thoughts of the person helps them to understand that they — not the situation — are in fact responsible for their actions.

> *Therapist:* Mom, when he went slamming out of the house and tore the screen, it sounds as though you thought to yourself, I'll get him for doing this, for tearing up the door and for yelling at me. He is such a monster I've got to slap it out of him. Is that what happened?

During the initial stage of establishing a therapeutic climate, it is important to use therapist statements that help family members see the relationship between their thoughts and behavior, but at this point, the cognitive elements of change are not the focus — that comes later in the treatment. Instead, it is important to begin laying the groundwork during the early stages of work with the family.

How Family Members Feel

An empathic relationship requires that each member involved feel understood, both in what is being said and what is being experienced affectively. The therapist, in responding to clients, identifies the affective state being experienced and helps to legitimize that the feelings are acceptable in the context being presented.

> *Therapist:* Mom, when he yells at you and slams out of the door [content of what the mother has said], you start thinking about how unfair he is and how he abuses you [cognitions of what the mother has said] and it really hurts; you get very angry. It sounds as though it is also very painful to not feel loved and cared for by him [affect of what the mother has said]. It seems that when you feel hurt and angry, those are the times you strike out and fight with him. Is that right?

Many family members have not had an opportunity to talk with a person who understands and accepts their affective states. Many are not even in touch with what they are feeling, as is evidenced by fathers, for example, who say they don't get mad, they just get even. Many people feel embarrassed about the affective responses they have toward their children, but understanding and accepting their emotional state is an important component of effective interventions with families.

Understanding Interactional Patterns

As discussed in Chapters 1 to 4, behavior does not occur in an isolated manner. Rather, the coercive interactional process is the core of dysfunctional families' problems. As the therapist initially works with the family, it is important to develop an understanding of the systemic properties of how each family member's interactions impact others. The behavior of an aggressive child in the family impacts the behavior of other members of the family, and subsequently they impact the aggressive child. Just as a situation impacts the thinking, feeling, and behavior of a person, so that person's behavior impacts the feelings, thoughts, and behaviors of others in the family context.

As may be seen in the following two diagrams, there are interactions within the individual as thoughts, feelings, and behavior interact and impact on the person, and within the family system there are interactions occurring among the members (see Figure 5.1 below). There is no linear cause-and-effect relationship in families (i.e., A causes B); rather, the relationship is reflected in a circularity which results in impacting each member in an ongoing pattern (i.e., A impacts B impacts A impacts B) (see Figure 5.2).

The therapist is responsible for helping members understand the interactional effect, for it is through breaking the cycle that family improvement occurs.

> *Therapist:* So Mom, when he yells and storms out, you feel hurt and angry. Then you slap him, which causes him to get so angry that he wants revenge because he thinks he shouldn't be hit. Then the power struggle just escalates, gets more and more painful, as each of you attempts to better the other. Then Dad steps in and starts fussing with you about not being able to control Billy, and Billy gets angry at him too for butting in on the fight. At that point all of you are involved. Is that how the interaction grows?

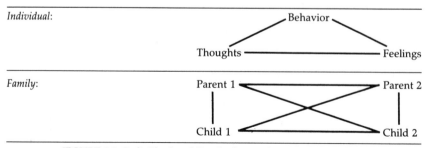

FIGURE 5.1. Individual and Family System Interaction Patterns.

Linear, Cause-and-Effect Relationship

A ——————→ B

Circular Family Relationship

FIGURE 5.2. Linear versus Circular Relationships.

IMPLEMENTING A POSITIVE
PROBLEM-SOLVING APPROACH

All families have problems and troublesome circumstances, but not all families have antisocial children or experience the painful interactions seen in families with oppositional-defiant- and conduct-disordered children. The characteristic that sets functional families apart from dysfunctional families is the ability to manage family problem solving (Fuelle, 1981; Glaser, 1989; Haubold, 1989; Horne, 1981; James, 1987). Often the approach taken by families reflects a deficit in ability to identify what the problem is, a failure to remain task-oriented once the problem is identified, an inability to develop alternative solutions for the problem, or a failure to engage in discussions with family members that will result in positive steps being taken. The result of poor problem-solving ability is that many families make the same mistakes over and over.

As a way of teaching effective positive problem solving, we model the process from the beginning.

Therapist: As you've described the situation, there seems to be a pattern, a pattern in which Billy misbehaves, then Mom and Dad get angry and yell, and then Billy becomes indignant and behaves even worse. It sounds as though the process goes on over and over. One of the things we do is take a look at the problem, identify what seems to be the basis of the conflict, and see if we can find other ways of handling it. You see, I'm not saying what you are doing is wrong, what I'm saying is that it doesn't seem to be working. When what we do doesn't work, it is important to back up a little and see if maybe we could approach the problem in a different way. I'm optimistic about working with you because our specialty here is helping to solve family problems, teaching family members ways they can approach problems so that they'll work out better.

At times, therapists become discouraged with the extent of problems presented by family members at the initial meeting. It is important that therapists remember to apply the problem-solving approach to their work with the family and not become overwhelmed with the conflict to the point that they become ineffective. Parallel process is a situation in which therapists have feelings related to a family that are the same as the family has toward an aggressive child or other situation. When this occurs, the therapist needs to attend to his or her affective state and realize that these feelings are providing direction for understanding what the family needs, assisting in clarifying the problem, and defining appropriate steps to take in addressing the problem.

UNDERSTANDING AND ADDRESSING RESISTANCE TO CHANGE

Resistant behaviors on the part of clients in therapy are blocks to the progress of treatment. Resistance may be a function of the therapist, the client(s), or the environment and is best addressed by a problem-solving approach that seeks to determine the function of the resistance and the process of removing it (Birchler, 1988).

Fleischman et al. (1983) discussed resistance as maintaining the status quo, putting the brakes on change which may be moving too rapidly, or a function of the therapist not being fully attuned to the client's needs. They suggest that resistance may be a comprehension problem rather than a lack of motivation. This may occur when the therapist uses language too sophisticated for the family, moves too quickly, covers too much material, doesn't provide sufficient examples or models and rehearsals, or leaves the family without adequate closure at the conclusion of therapy. Further, they report that the therapist must relate tasks of therapy to client goals and be certain that clients see the relationship of tasks to outcome goals. They also discuss modifying tasks and assignments so that goals can be more adequately met. ʼ

As discussed earlier, therapists should work to prevent the emergence of resistance by providing an office environment conducive to feeling secure and comfortable and by offering relationship skills that lead to comfort with the therapeutic process. Birchler (1988) has defined processes the therapist may use to facilitate participation by family members:

1. Modeling good listening behavior
2. Regulating and balancing the verbal participation of each family member

3. Recognizing and allowing for each partner's ventilation of negative feelings
4. Providing a clear rationale regarding procedures
5. Obtaining an explicit commitment from the family. (pp. 138–139)

These steps are consistent with the work of Jacobson and Margolin (1979), who indicated that a collaborative set needs to be established in order to facilitate therapy and reduce resistance. This collaborative set occurs when family members move away from blaming others for problems in the family and adopt a problem-solving approach that recognizes the interactional effect of the family conflict. The focus is on relationship enhancement (i.e., win-win) rather than on the individual approach (i.e., win-lose) that most family members bring to therapy.

It is best to prevent resistance from developing by initiating a therapeutic alliance that leads to positive efforts on the part of all involved. This is not always possible, and once resistance emerges, it is best to address it directly rather than attempt to work around it. Family members may fail to follow through or stop participating in activities related to therapy for a number of reasons, and it is the therapist's responsibility to attempt to define the nature of this problem.

One area in which resistance often develops is related to cognitive issues. A parent or child with a belief system that is counterproductive to the therapeutic approach will not cooperate with treatment unless the issues are discussed and clarified. For example, a parent who believes an antisocial child can never change, who has negative feelings for a child, or who has religious convictions contrary to the therapy model will need to have these issues addressed. One way of doing this is to ask the parent to engage in an "as if" process for a short time.

> *Therapist:* I realize, Mr. Jones, that you think children should be spanked for misbehaving, that the "spare the rod, spoil the child" rule should be enforced frequently. At the same time, the problems have gotten worse each year, to the point that Liz is now in trouble at home, at school, and in the community. What I'd like to suggest is that you give us a try, act as if the process will work. Do this for a few weeks. Try it. You see, the nice thing about this approach is that if it doesn't work, you can always go back to the way you have been doing things, and with no loss because Liz is already misbehaving more than you wish. Then you'll have two ways of approaching the problem — the spanking you've been doing and the discipline we review.

Although the therapist may address resistance early through efforts to prevent it (e.g., relationship development, goal setting, establishing a positive problem-solving orientation) and through direct attention to it during therapy (e.g., discussing it, reframing or redefining it), attention must also be directed toward environmental circumstances that may produce it. Environmental resistance occurs when people are more influenced outside therapy not to change than they are in therapy to change. For example, gang members may exert more influence on an adolescent than the family is able to within the home setting, and family members (e.g., grandparents, aunts, and uncles) or neighbors and/or friends may ridicule the family for receiving treatment.

Environmental issues are best dealt with just as other forms of resistance are: directly discussing them and attempting to address the problems. A discussion of the positive benefits of treatment may help overcome external influences, and in-session rehearsals of ways to respond to and manage the coercive influence of friends and family members are helpful. For adolescents who are strongly influenced by peers, it is sometimes necessary to increase the stakes for staying in therapy through such efforts as raising allowances, restricting access to privileges, and even potentially relying on placement in a group or foster home or juvenile correctional facility.

ESTABLISHING RELATIONSHIPS WITH SCHOOL AND AGENCY PERSONNEL

Although the primary source of change and improvement in the treatment of conduct- and oppositional-defiant-disordered children is through a family intervention, relationships with other systems that interact with the child are also very important. For the last decade of treating behavior-disordered children, more than half of all referrals have come from school personnel, whereas smaller numbers have been from CPS of the welfare department, the juvenile court and the juvenile center, church personnel, or mental health personnel. Good mental health practice calls for establishing and maintaining effective relationships with referral sources to obtain an ongoing source of clients and, more importantly, for developing therapeutic approaches that provide the greatest opportunity for change.

Working with Schools

School personnel are the ones who are on the front line with children, seeing them usually for longer periods each day than parents do. They are able to observe ways in which children interact with others and document aggressiveness that exceeds the normal limits expected in the classroom. Our experience is that teachers care about their students and want them to benefit from services that will allow them to be more effective learners.

Within the school setting the person most likely to make referrals for treatment is the school counselor. This is particularly true at the secondary level, because nationwide statistics show that this is the school level most likely to have a counselor. Our school community has counselors in the elementary schools, as well as at the secondary level, and they have developed a prevention approach in which they attempt to address problems before they have fully developed. This results in the counselor working with children earlier than the secondary level and making referrals before problems become too unmanageable. Usually the counselor has worked with the student and attempted to facilitate changes within the school setting but has been unsuccessful. The counselor may provide information about the types of behaviors occurring and is able to make available interactional data which will be useful in understanding the problems of the family.

We work with counselors to aid them in knowing how to make referrals, particularly ways in which to present therapy to parents so that the service will be seen as a cooperative approach to helping rather than a punitive assignment for having an aggressive child.

When referrals are made by school personnel, it is important to schedule meetings to identify the nature of the problem, decide how much support will be offered by the school, and determine how much teachers will be able to participate in activities requiring teacher support, such as completing behavior checklists and filling out daily report cards. We have found teachers, counselors, and principals to be most helpful and cooperative when they find that their students are involved in our treatment program and that the approach to helping children will be a collaborative effort. Of course, the same therapist skills used with a family are also used with school personnel, including being empathic, demonstrating support, and utilizing a positive problem-solving approach.

Working with Agencies

Most of the guidelines related to working with schools also apply to agencies. Agencies, though, do not become involved with children unless a problem has already escalated to a level where intervention is not considered preventative but is remedial. At the point of referral, the agency is usually in a coercive relationship with the family. Also, there is generally less involvement in a therapeutic alliance approach — juvenile courts want the child "fixed" and don't want to be involved, and

CPS desires that the child no longer need its involvement. The most effective way to function with agency personnel is to work cooperatively, define the problem, and provide regular feedback. It is more difficult, however, to have active therapeutic involvement.

Chapter 6

Preparing for Success: Environmental Intervention

INTRODUCING THE FAUX FAMILY

The Faux Family (Boyer & Horne, 1988; Horne, Boyer, Sayger, & Passmore, 1988, October) was referred for treatment by the Child Protective Services (CPS) division of the local welfare department. The referral report form is presented in Figure 6.1 on page 76.

In Figure 6.2 (on page 77) all family members identified by the label "Therapy" initially participated in the treatment. Nick originally indicated he would not be involved in the therapy program because he did not live in the household and was not in need of services. Because he was involved with Cara and was the father of her unborn child, CPS applied pressure through threat of legal action, because of abuse to a minor (Jimmy) and contributing to the delinquency of a minor (Cara), if he refused to participate. Nick remained involved with the family for only three sessions and then quit the community, leaving no forwarding information.

DEFINING THE PROBLEM

During the initial meeting with the family the objective was to define the problem areas that had caused the family to become involved in treatment. This was a delicate process because the way the family defined the problem initially was not likely to be the way the therapist conceptualized it. Most often parents present the problem as a behavioral dysfunction on the part of the child. But, as described in earlier chapters, the child's behavior is a function of his or her interactions with family members, peers, teachers, and others. As the problem(s) is presented, the therapist redefines it in interactional, systemic terms.

75

Client name:	Terri Faux	Caseworker:	Smith
Address:	Main Street	Referral date:	1/12/90
	Middletown, USA		
Telephone:	None		
Children:	Cara Doe, 16	School: Left, 10/89	
	Jimmy Faux, 11	Middletown Elementary	
	Evan Faux, 9	Middletown Elementary	

Reason for referral: Neglect _____
                 Physical abuse __X___
                 Sexual abuse _____

Case status: Informal adjustment __X___
                 Placement _____

Type of service: Preplacement preventive __X___
                 Reunification _____

Address of children if placed out of home: __NA_

CPS case synopsis:

This case came to the attention of CPS when Jimmy was taken to the emergency room of the Middletown Hospital with bruises following a fight with Nick, the boyfriend of Cara. Emergency room physicians reported the case, expressing concern for the welfare of Jimmy.

Jimmy has a history of aggressive behavior at school and frequently engages in fights and arguments with other children. He has a reputation for having a short temper and poor emotional control. He has a poor academic record and has been retained in school once.

Evan also has behavior problems and fights at school and also with Jimmy. He has academic problems but overall performs better at school than Jimmy.

Cara has a history of being belligerent and argumentative. She performed poorly at school and left school when she reached 16. She has been arrested twice for shoplifting. She is six months pregnant by her current boyfriend, Nick. Cara and Nick's relationship has been violent since her pregnancy was confirmed. The fight Nick and Jimmy had was a result of Jimmy attempting to stop Nick from physically shoving Cara. Nick became violent with Jimmy and began beating on him.

The children live at home with Terri, the mother, and with the maternal grandmother (Lynne) and Terri's live-in boyfriend, Jake. Terri appears to be overwhelmed and has difficulty providing consistent parenting to her children. Lynne and Jake are both involved with Terri in the parenting.

The family has had no prior CPS involvement and is not currently involved with other social service agencies, other than for Cara having to report each month to a probation officer for her shoplifting episodes.

FIGURE 6.1. Home-Based Family Therapy Referral.

This requires understanding the antecedents to and the consequences of problems, as well as the circularity of the antecedents and consequences in maintaining dysfunctional systems. This stage of treatment involves helping all members of the family understand the process of coercion and how conflict escalates.

When the Faux family was referred by CPS, an appointment was set at a time when the entire family could be present. A 2-hour interview

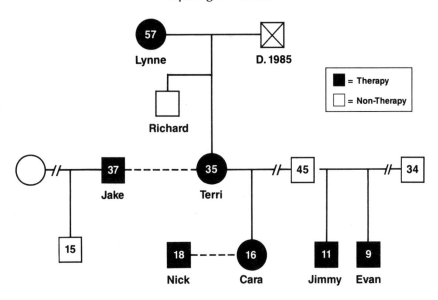

FIGURE 6.2. The Faux family constellation.

period was scheduled, and a cotherapy approach was selected. Cotherapists can function very effectively with a chaotic family such as the Fauxes because often one person is needed to observe interactions as the other attempts to provide interventions. Further, members of a family such as this will need to be separated in order to interview different elements of the family system such as parents, children, or Cara alone. Also, one therapist may work with one unit of the family (children) while the other conducts assessment procedures with another unit (parents).

The initial involvement with the Faux family demonstrated quickly that separation of family members would be important. Lynne was openly hostile about Terri's lack of parenting skills, and she clearly disapproved of Terri's live-in boyfriend, Jake, whom she thought should not be disciplining the children because he was not their father.

Terri seemed overwhelmed by the entire gathering and appeared depressed, lethargic, and somewhat distant. On prompting, she did express anger about being required to be in therapy because of "problems that aren't mine," saying, "Nick shouldn't have hit Jimmy."

Jake appeared to be the most cooperative of all in the gathering, indicating that the family needed help because there appeared to be lots of problems and they were getting worse instead of better. Jake said he had tried to do lots of things, but there was little support and people kept undercutting his attempts, particularly Lynne, whom Jake felt "babied" the children too much. He also thought she didn't follow through on threats and punishment.

Jimmy appeared to be quite reluctant to be at the session and was noncooperative. He didn't answer questions about his behavior until the incident with Nick was presented, at which time he became visibly angry. He thought Nick should not be allowed in the house because he often hit Cara and the two boys, bossed Terri around, and used alcohol and drugs around the house.

Evan was cute and curious about the experience of being in therapy. He wanted to know whether he could watch himself on the television monitor and was quite impressed with the clinic setting, which is on the 14th floor of a 15-story building. The problem he reported was being the smallest in the family and being bullied by all the other family members.

Cara was noncooperative and sullen and expressed strong reservations about being in therapy. She said she thought it would be a waste of time and that the only thing that would happen would be that Lynne, Terri, and Jake would all complain about her not being in school and being pregnant by Nick.

Nick was openly hostile about being in therapy and reported that he didn't intend to stay. He thought his rights were being abused because he hadn't been found guilty of breaking any law and therefore should not be forced to do something he didn't want to do. It was pointed out that he had the option of not participating, but that we would then have no control over what would happen between him and the courts because CPS had required his participation.

During the session, the family constellation was subdivided a number of times to provide family members more opportunity to discuss their concerns. This was done to make certain that the interview would not become a sounding board of complaints and criticisms by the parents against the children, one that the children would have to sit through. When children have to remain in an aversive clinical setting and listen to all their antisocial behaviors being reviewed, they become noncooperative and assume the therapist is aligning with the parents because she or he sits and listens to the presentation.

It is important that children have the opportunity to discuss with the therapist changes they would like to see happen in their family. This serves three purposes: (a) The child feels listened to, validated, and understood; (b) The therapist develops a picture of the family functioning (and dysfunctioning) from the child's perspective; and (c) The therapist can use the child's requests for change at a later date to elicit cooperation in activities in which the child may not want to participate — for example, when the child does not want to do time-out but in the initial interview reported that he wanted his mother to quit screaming at him.

> *Therapist:* So, Jimmy, you said you wanted your Mom to quit screaming at you, but now you don't want to do time-out. I'll tell you what, let's try the time-out and see if it isn't better than being screamed at.

For the Faux family the following problems were defined:

1. A need for more effective and coordinated parenting, including negotiating roles and responsibilities, by the adults in the family
2. Childhood discipline for Jimmy and Evan, including addressing issues around the home, at school, and in the community (e.g., eating out at fast-food places, going to shopping centers)
3. Improved academic performances for Jimmy and Evan
4. Improved communication between Terri, Jake, and Lynne, with the need to negotiate effective boundaries for discipline, household management, and responsibilities
5. Attention to Cara's situation, with her not being aware of effective prenatal care for her child, having a poor academic history, and lacking employment skills; also, a need to address the violent nature of the relationship between Cara and Nick so that a nonviolent means of disagreement could be reached.

A number of ancillary problem areas were noted, including Terri's depression and the financial state of the family (viz., Lynne had a limited retirement income, Jake was employed but did not earn much money, and Terri was employed as a waitress, but her depression and family problems were interfering with her performance).

The nature of the family functioning was a reflection of both poor family and general living skills. The family members interacted through coercive and punishing processes that led to a constant cycle of anger and revenge, with people feeling they were being treated unfairly and responding to the perceived unfair situation by striking out in the immediate circumstances or seeking revenge at a later date. The family expressed considerable externality of responsibility, indicating that other people were responsible for the problems, either in the family ("If Nick would just leave us alone") or external to the family ("If the hospital just wouldn't have called Welfare none of this would be happening. We can handle our problems"). The external locus of responsibility was also directed toward performance in other areas, such as school ("The boys aren't bad; if the other kids just would leave them alone, they wouldn't be having trouble at school" or "The teachers don't like the Faux family, and so they don't help our kids like they do other kids.

That's why they have trouble") and employment ("It doesn't matter what you do, the boss decides what happens to you").

In discussing the problems with the family, the therapists defined two areas for initial intervention, the boys' discipline and helping Cara identify ways of making some changes in her life.

> *Therapist:* We've discussed a number of problem areas for your family, a number of ways you would like to see your family act differently. This includes helping the boys to get along better at home, mind you better, and it includes helping them do better at school. Another area is related to who is going to be in charge of discipline for the boys, and this is an adult issue that needs to be talked about. Still another topic is how Cara gets along in the family: her fighting with the boys, not wanting to mind the adults, and not having a plan for preparing herself for motherhood or for employment. A couple of other areas of concern are how depressed Terri gets and the difficulty making ends meet with the amount of money that's available. What we'd like to suggest is that we start with a couple of areas, work on them for a few weeks, and then reassess where we are. What we'd like to suggest is that we zero in on Jimmy and Evan — how to help them learn to mind you better and ways to get them doing a little better in school. The second area is in working with Cara and Nick to see if we can come up with some ideas on how they might get along better with each other and see if we can help Cara find information about caring for herself and the baby. Do those two ideas sound like a direction you'd like to take?

At this point it becomes very important to review therapy components with the family. A discussion of the time involved, the nature of the treatment, which involves having family members perform tasks between sessions, the follow-through with family and school contacts by the therapist, and any expenses involved. Also at this point, the theoretical implications of treatment need to be addressed, including the notion that changing children involves having all family members make some changes.

> *Therapist:* One thing we've noticed in treating many families is that in order to help children make the changes that are wanted, it is often necessary for parents to make some changes too. For example, sometimes kids hit each other, and the parents get upset about that. But sometimes parents hit people too — like their children — and so the children learn that hitting is okay. So we may have to come up with some ideas about how you may need to do things a little differently so that Jimmy can see that you are working at the family problems too. Does that seem reasonable?

ESTABLISHING GOALS

Once the family has been interviewed and specific areas to be addressed have been identified and discussed, it is important to develop clear, definable, achievable goals. In establishing goals we use a goal setting form (Figure 6.3).

Goal Setting Form

Family _____   Therapist _____   Date _____

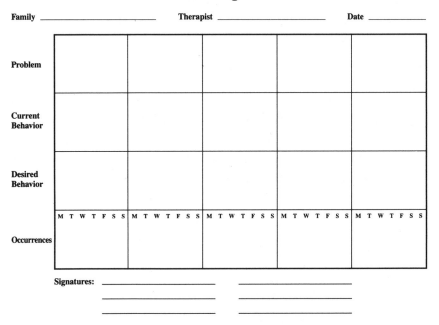

Signatures:

FIGURE 6.3. Goal Setting Form.

This form is designed to identify five problem areas and was developed for use with one problem child in a family. For the Faux family, the form in Figure 6.4 was completed (on page 82).

After the goal form has been completed, with all family members present, the therapist reviews the goals and explains that it is necessary to observe the extent of the problem. Each problem is reviewed, and it is explained who will monitor whether or not the behavior occurred during the week. An example is demonstrated so that all members of the family understand how to use the form to record whether or not an incident occurred.

ESTABLISHING FAMILY
GUIDELINES FOR POSITIVE
CHANGE

After the problem areas to be addressed have been reviewed with the family, it is important to move toward defining ways to improve family functioning as a way of alleviating the problems defined on the

Goal Setting Form

Family __Faux (Jimmy)__   Therapist __Jane Doe__   Date __1/19/89__

	Cooperation	Language	Not Minding	Room	School
Problem					
Current Behavior	Daily fights with Evan, argues with all family members on a daily basis, talks back.	Uses profanity when angry, curses Evan during fights or arguments.	Does about 3 out of 10 things he is told to do.	Never picks up clothes, toys; does not make bed.	Skips school; fights at school; poor grades.
Desired Behavior	Replaces fighting with cooperation. Replaces arguing with cooperation, compliance. Ends talking back.	Speaks pleasantly, with friendly voice. No profanity.	Complies with 8 out of 10 things he is told to do.	Keeps room straight (clothes, toys, bed) 5 days per week.	Attends school, absent no more than once per semester.
Occurrences	M T W T F S S	M T W T F S S	M T W T F S S	M T W T F S S	M T W T F S S

Signatures: *Jimmy Faux*
Terri Faux
_____   _____
_____   _____

FIGURE 6.4. Goals for the Faux family.

goal sheet. There are some specific steps that are introduced early in the treatment process.

Consistency and Persistence

One area where families with conduct- or oppositional-defiant-disordered children experience considerable difficulty is in being consistent in their efforts. A lack of predictability often permeates the family environment. The children know that if they misbehave, they are likely to be successful in getting away with the misbehavior but that at some point very coercive action will be taken.

Therapist: Evan, it seems your mother tells you to turn off the television and get ready for bed, but you don't follow through on that very well. I'm wondering why not?
Evan: I do.
Therapist: You turn off the TV and go to bed everytime your mom tells you to? I thought she had to ask you several times to turn off the TV.
Evan: She does. She gets really mad after awhile.
Therapist: Do you know when she's going to get mad?

Evan: Yes, you can tell by her voice. She tells me and tells me, and then she tells me like she means it.

One of the most difficult ideas parents must understand is the old expression: *Say what you mean and mean what you say.* Helping Terri learn to tell Evan to turn off the TV with one statement is difficult but necessary:

Therapist: Terri, Evan has learned over the years that you don't mean a lot of what you say; he knows you aren't likely to do anything if he doesn't follow through with what you tell him to do. I guess one way of looking at the situation is that you've taught him to not mind you until you start getting truly agitated. Is that what you meant to do?
Terri: No.
Therapist: I didn't think so. The best way to handle the problem is to consider what you are about to say, to think about whether you really mean what you say. If you don't mean it, I wouldn't say it. Let's practice a few situations now and see how you can use these ideas.

Concreteness and Clarity of Instructions

A second area where families with oppositional-defiant- and conduct-disordered children have difficulty is in making clear requests or commands. Parents frequently talk about having their children "behave" or "mind" or "be good," but these expressions are usually so diffuse that neither the parent nor the child knows what is meant by them. Parents often tell children to "straighten up" or "cut it out" without being very specific about what is expected of them or without getting the child's attention before making a request. Although expressions like these may be useful and even functional in average families not experiencing the high level of coercion and pain that aggressive families do, the vagueness of the expressions provides loopholes for the antisocial child to slip through.

We teach parents to specify what they expect from their child by explicitly stating what they want done, when they want it done, and how they want it done. For example,

I want you to turn off the TV at 9:00 and go to bed.
When this television show is over, I want you to come to dinner.
After dinner I want you to clear the table and take out the garbage. Do that before you go out to play again.

Show Respect and Dignity

One of the difficulties families with aggressive children have is expressing positive caring. One guideline that we try to teach all family members is to treat each other even better than family — treat each other like strangers.

Therapist: Dad, I noted that when I asked you how you would tell Jimmy to not walk in with muddy shoes, you said, "Don't be stupid. Don't walk in here with mud on your shoes or I'll beat your tail." I'm wondering, if a stranger — or maybe a neighbor or friend — came to your door with muddy shoes, how would you handle the situation?

Client: I'd tell them not to come in with muddy shoes, to please clean the mud off or to take the shoes off before coming in.

Therapist: Could you tell Jimmy that, with the same kindness in your voice you just used, so that he would know that you don't want a muddy floor but that you do care about him?

Client: Yes, I could, but he ought to know better.

Therapist: True, he should. But so should your friend or neighbor, and yet you use a kind tone of voice to tell them. What I'm asking of you is that you treat Jimmy as well as you would someone who isn't a member of the family.

Fairness

When we conduct the initial interview with the family and spend time with the adolescent or child, a constant theme we hear is that their family isn't fair to them. They complain that because the adults are grown, they think they can treat children any way they want and that situations occur that aren't fair. Many of the circumstances they complain about are a function of age and maturity (e.g., adults do get to stay up later at night), but often they make a very good point — in aggressive or antisocial families the parents often are unfair. In one of our examinations of family interactions comparing effective families with dysfunctional families, it was observed that functional families engaged in fair and reasonable activities more than dysfunctional families did. This was particularly true for issues of responsibility: Functional mothers were responsible for parent roles and held children responsible for child roles (e.g., Mom would do the wash and prepare dinner but would hold the child responsible for schoolwork and for getting up in the morning), whereas in dysfunctional families mothers would often unfairly blame the child for problems. We have experienced even high-level antisocial adolescents who have identified as one of their goals that they be treated fairly at home, and they often are accurate in their appraisal of the family environment as operating unfairly.

ANTICIPATING PROBLEMS

A characteristic of families with oppositional-defiant- or conduct-disordered children is that they are not very effective at anticipating problems. Antisocial behavior usually has identifiable preceding circumstances. Often parents of aggressive children are able to identify the development of aggressive behavior in children from other families but are not very effective in making the same observations about their own children, even when there are clear antecedents indicating trouble is about to develop.

> *Therapist:* So Terri, one area where you frequently have trouble with Jimmy and Evan is at the grocery store. They both seem inclined to have temper tantrums and demand candy or something else, and you get angry and a scene develops. It is interesting to note, as you described the situation, that you pick them up after school and go grocery shopping. Do you ever have a snack or anything for them in the car before going to the store?
>
> *Terri:* No, I don't. Why?
>
> *Therapist:* Well, I've noticed that even for adults, who have good control, it may be difficult to go through a grocery store without wanting something. I think this would be especially true for a young person who has spent six or more hours in school, is tired, and sees a lot of tempting foods. I'm wondering if one way to handle this problem may be to prevent it from happening in the first place. What if we consider a couple of alternatives. First, let's consider finding a way to not take the kids to the store. Could they stay home with Lynne? The second alternative would be, after explaining to them that they can't have a temper tantrum and that you won't be buying them anything in the store, that you will let them know you will provide them with a snack before going into the store. Do you think that might help solve the problem?

Parents of antisocial children frequently are unable to recognize the relationship between what they do and the conflicts that develop. Problems that are prevented from occurring are much easier to manage than problems that have erupted into a full-blown conflict. One way to address this issue is to spend time talking with the parents and have them identify the sequence of problems that occur in the home. Then, problem-solve together to see if there are ways of anticipating difficulties and cutting them off before they arise. Another step in this process is to work with the children involved and have them help identify steps that need to be taken to prevent problems from developing.

> *Therapist:* Evan, do you have some ideas about things that could be done differently around the house so that there would be fewer problems?
>
> *Evan:* If the TV wasn't right outside my room I could go to sleep better and I wouldn't keep trying to sneak out and watch it.

Some of the solutions to problems are very obvious and can be handled very easily with an outside perspective on the relationship between the problem and the environmental influences that maintain the problem. With the Faux family, for example, one difficulty was in getting the two boys to bed. They shared a room, but Jimmy wanted to stay up later at night and Evan would frequently complain about the differential bedtime. Further, they had difficulty keeping their things apart, so that there were frequent arguments about personal space issues. At the same time, the family had a bedroom which was used as a playroom for the two boys where games, toys, and other items were located. A number of conflicts disappeared when Evan was given this room as a separate bedroom.

HELPING PARENTS

Stress and pain are clearly evident in families with antisocial children, particularly in parents who, as adults, assume they should know how to manage children but clearly are having difficulty with the process. Two areas in particular need of attention for parents are enhancing their relationship with one another and enhancing positive extrafamilial social contacts.

Enhancing the Couple's Relationship

If there are two parents in the family (as in the Faux family, even though Terri and Jake are not married nor is Jake the father of the children), the probability is high that their marital relationship will need therapeutic attention. Our experience is that the parents generally have devoted their energy to the child, by fighting and arguing, or have quit attending to each other by having one go to the tavern while the other is left alone. We specifically address the couple's relationship and help them identify ways in which they would like to improve how they function as adults together. We discuss with the couple how much time they spend together and whether it is enjoyable or unpleasant. We have them discuss how they would like their time together to be different. Generally we begin making assignments for the couple to practice.

> *Therapist:* Terri, you and Jake seemed to have had some pretty good times in the past, but you don't seem to be enjoying each other's company as much any more. Why is that?
>
> *Terri:* It's because whenever we're home the boys are always doing something or that damned Nick is around or my mom is on my case about what I'm not doing right as a mother.
>
> *Therapist:* It seems you two need some time, then? Let's talk about how you might get together. What would you think of the two of you working out with Lynne that maybe one night a week you and Jake might go out together. Even if it doesn't cost much money, you could spend some time together, maybe walking through the park, or now in the summer fixing a picnic just for the two of you. It also sounds as though you and Lynne don't get to spend any time together that doesn't revolve around fighting with or about the kids. Would you like to explore some options on how the two of you might be able to spend some special time together each week without the hassles of the kids around?

Many adults develop a life-style pattern that deprives them of engaging in some of the very activities that would help them manage their problems better, and it becomes the responsibility of the therapist to help identify ways in which they can renew their support and caring for one another.

There are a number of specific activities that may be of use to parents in helping them to improve their relationship, including caring days (Stuart, 1980) where each partner chooses one day of the week on which he or she is asked to engage in caring behaviors, such as doing the dishes or listening to the spouse discuss problems or other topics of interest. Or they may be taught a homework assignment designed to catch the spouse doing or saying something nice and let them know that the behavior is appreciated and prized (Liberman, Wheeler, & Sanders, 1976).

Enhancing Positive Social Contacts

Many parents, mothers in particular, experience what Wahler (1980) has referred to as "insularity." They become insulated from adult and outside contacts as a result of their becoming encapsulated by family problems. Wahler found that mothers who had contacts with other people outside the home did much better in family improvement, even if the contact itself was somewhat aversive, than mothers who did not have such contacts. Szykula, Mas, Turner, Crowley, and Sayger (1989) have noted that prosocial interactions between mothers and their children are positively correlated with pleasurable extrafamilial contacts. Thus, establishing a positive adult cohort for parents of conduct- and oppositional-defiant-disordered children can be an integral part of a successful treatment program.

Steps that help adults find ways of establishing positive social contacts can at times be very difficult, particularly given the limited financial resources so many families have and the time limitations for parents given the busy lives they lead working with children. We have found a number of possibilities, however, including:

1. Getting out for coffee with a friend, or having a friend over to visit
2. Doing volunteer work during the school day when the children are away from the home
3. Seeking part- or full-time employment
4. Enrolling in a job-training, vocational, educational or personal growth experience.

Helping parents, particularly mothers, enhance their self-confidence and self-esteem is a major focus of treatment. Parents who lack self-efficacy and who are not comfortable with their abilities are less likely to be able to follow through with change.

EMPHASIZING A PROBLEM-SOLVING APPROACH

An approach developed and used from the beginning of treatment through to the end is a positive problem-solving approach. As reflected in many of the guidelines developed above, parents of antisocial children generally are not very effective problem solvers: They are unable to see the relationship between the behavior they object to and conditions occurring in the home and in their interactions. The following chapters, which describe the treatment intervention in more detail, demonstrate how the problem-solving approach is incorporated into all phases of the treatment program, including addressing how the therapist will use the model to manage therapeutic issues that develop.

Chapter 7
Managing Self and Others

A characteristic of families with antisocial children is a lack of self-control. Members of aggressive families have more difficulty with behavioral control skills than those of average families (Fuelle, 1981; Glaser, 1989; Haubold, 1989; Horne, 1981; James, 1987; P. W. Morris et al., 1988; Patterson, 1982). The common belief that oppositional or conduct problems on the part of a child or young adolescent represent a form of rebellion against an otherwise well-functioning family does not hold up under the scrutiny of family observations. There are some exceptions to this generalization, including evidence from research on sibling positions, which indicates that a child who cannot adequately find his or her place in the family may likely become the family "black sheep." This child tends to act out as a way of finding a role in an otherwise well-functioning family constellation (Lowe, 1982). Our work with conduct- and oppositional-defiant-disordered children referred for treatment has led to the conclusion that aggression is generally not isolated within one individual family member but is a family characteristic. In such families, as Lederer and Jackson (1968) stated, "Nastiness begets nastiness" (p. 269).

Aggressive behavior is not the only way family members may demonstrate a lack of effective self-control. Just as anger explosions or temper tantrums represent a lack of ability to adequately respond to a situation, so depression, resignation, or apathy also indicates an inability to handle life circumstances in a responsible manner.

PARENTAL SELF-CONTROL
SKILLS

It is very important to address parental self-control early in the treatment program. Parents who lack effective self-control for themselves are not able to model the behavior for their children, and without an appropriate model, children will not be able to develop the behavioral skill. Parents who are able to discipline only by yelling, hitting, or screaming are not able to help their children learn responsible ways of handling disappointments or conflicts. Conversely, a mother who becomes depressed and melancholy over the seemingly insurmountable problems presented by children who refuse to obey and withdraws from the parenting role is (a) admitting defeat to herself and her children, (b) failing to provide an effective role model for the children, and (c) teaching the children that they are more powerful than she is and that they may have their way if they escalate their misbehavior to a sufficient level.

In families with antisocial children, the children generally have effectively wrested power from the parents so that the parents are ineffective in their attempts to make them mind, obey, or comply with parental requests. Out of frustration, then, parents resort to acting out aggressively themselves in order to make their points, or just give up and allow the children free reign to do as they please. Both are irresponsible and ineffective directions for the parents to take but represent their lack of knowing what else to do. In working with clinical families, even families in which there has been abuse and neglect, a guiding belief we hold is that parents are doing the best they know how to do under the circumstances they are experiencing. Parents are not purposefully cruel or mean; rather, their repertoire of skills is deficient when it comes to knowing how to effectively parent their children. This is an optimistic approach to working with families and provides the opportunity to help parents learn more effective parenting skills and apply these skills in a manner that will not involve aggressive, hostile, or depressed interactions with their children.

In the Faux family, lack of self-control skills was evident in all members of the family, but these skills were particularly lacking in the adults. The grandmother, Lynne, would tell her daughter, Terri, how she thought the children should be disciplined, but if Terri disagreed or failed to follow through, Lynne would withdraw and become pouty and noncooperative. She would appear to be hurt by having her suggestions ignored and would allow the children to do as they pleased rather than deal directly with Terri or the children about the issue.

Terri was overwhelmed by the behavior of the children, and her pattern of parenting was to nag them, remind them constantly of what was expected of them, and threaten them with groundings and/or spankings. When she was ignored over a period of time, she would strike out at the particular offending child with yelling, spanking, or other excessive displays of anger. Terri would feel guilty about the harshness of her behavior and ignore the next series of behaviors, or even at times apologize and tell the children they were right and she was wrong. She also would become depressed about her inability to manage the children and would withdraw from attending to them.

Jake, who was the live-in boyfriend, did not feel he should be doing much to discipline the children because he was not their father and wasn't married to Terri. He would get angry with the children and at times would attempt to discipline them, especially when Terri was depressed and didn't seem capable of managing the situation. He would occasionally drink an excessive amount of alcohol and become almost abusive in his disciplinary actions toward the children, after which Terri and Lynne would become upset with him and tell him to leave the kids alone.

SELF-CONTROL METHODS FOR PARENTS

A number of methods have been developed for helping parents learn more positive control methods as replacements for anger or depression.

Developing a Positive Problem-solving Approach

One reason for loss of control by adults is the belief that a problem has a single solution and that they know how to solve it. Our research has indicated just the opposite — dysfunctional families are not effective problem solvers. Parents in dysfunctional families experience considerable difficulty in the management of problems because they continue to apply disciplinary methods that do not work. They are like a person who has lost an object and doesn't know where it is but keeps looking in the same places over and over — they know the object is not there but they don't know where else to look and so they keep returning to the same ineffective solution. So it is with parents of antisocial children — they know that what they are doing does not work, but they are unable to see any alternatives.

Frequently there are payoffs for their continued practice — spanking a child often causes the child to stop the misbehavior in the immediate situation but does not stop the behavior from recurring:

> *Terri:* I just don't know what to do. Every time Jimmy gets in a fight at school I spank him and send him to his room. He just yells at me and tells me he doesn't care, and he is back in just a little while doing just whatever he wants to. I spank him all the time, but it doesn't seem to make any difference, and I don't know what else to do.

> *Therapist:*   So you spank him a lot, but he just continues to misbehave. He has demonstrated to you that the spankings won't work, so we now need to begin to consider other directions, other steps that may be taken.

To help parents understand the positive problem-solving approach, we use a modified version of the questions developed by Glasser (1972) for his reality therapy treatment approach.

1. What is your goal?
2. What are you doing?
3. Is what you are doing helping you to achieve your goal?
4. What could you do differently?

Because in earlier sessions the family members have received help in defining the goal(s) they have set for the family, the therapist is able to use this information in the problem-solving stage to help parents identify what they want in their relationship(s) with their kids. The process would proceed along these lines:

> *Therapist:*   Terri, you've indicated that the goal you have is to have the children mind you better. But when you get angry and upset you yell at them, and the result is that you feel bad and they still don't mind you very well. Eventually the problem escalates until you spank them, and then you feel guilty and they feel revengeful, and no one is satisfied. So, the goal is to get along better with the children, right?
>
> *Terri:*   Yes, but . . . .
>
> *Therapist:*   So then we say, What is your goal? It is to get along better. Then the next question is, What are you doing? You are finding yourself getting angry, upset, wanting to spank the kids. That's what you are doing. Right?
>
> *Terri:*   Yes, I do get angry and start wanting to tear into them.
>
> *Therapist:*   Then the third question, Does that help you to achieve your goal? That is, when you get angry and want to tear into them, does that help you get along better?
>
> *Terri:*   Of course not.
>
> *Therapist:*   Okay, and so that is what we need to look at next. What do you need to do differently?
>
> *Terri:*   I don't know. If I knew, I probably wouldn't be having so much trouble controlling my anger. I'd get along better and wouldn't have to spank them.
>
> *Therapist:*   Right, and that's the next step we're going to begin exploring, what else you can do. There are a number of specific activities, and we're going to go over them now so that you will have more options.

This process is very important, as it demonstrates to parents steps to be taken in becoming more effective problem solvers. Further, it introduces steps that will allow them to step back from the crisis situation and engage in a reasoning activity that allows a calmer method for handling the problem. We keep the four questions on laminated 3×5 cards which we give to each member of the family as we go over the steps. For a large family, such as the Fauxes, it is important to go through the entire process with all family members, including the children.

Relaxation Training

A second step in the process of teaching parents effective self-control skills involves helping them learn to better control their bodily response to situations that normally lead to their becoming upset. There are a number of effective relaxation training methods available, ranging from the very detailed and elaborate, which take weeks to master, to very brief steps. We choose to use a brief calming response approach for several reasons. First, relaxation is not our primary focus, so we do not want to spend an inordinate amount of time on it. Second, we have found that the brief intervention is about as effective as more detailed training. And third, parents respond more favorably to the briefer intervention and see immediate applications which they often do not see in the more extended training approaches.

The steps in a brief calming responding pattern include the following:

> *Therapist:*   Terri, what I want you to do is close your eyes, get as comfortable as you can, and then inhale as fully as possible. As you inhale, think the word "calm." When you have inhaled as fully as you can, slowly count upward, one, two, three, and so on, until you begin to feel discomfort. Then exhale as fully as you can, and as you do so, think the word "relax" as you let the air out. With all the air out, I want you to again begin counting, one, two, three, and so on, until you again begin to feel a sense of discomfort. Then repeat the process again. Continue to do this for 3 to 5 minutes.

While this does not provide a deep relaxation state, it does serve two purposes: (a) it slows down the person and creates a calming effect, and (b) it stops negative interactions, particularly those that have begun escalating in a coercive cycle. Parents report that this method is easily mastered, has an immediate impact, and even generalizes to other settings. Some clients have reported that they use the skill at work as well as at home and experience more positive interactions with colleagues and supervisors as a result of being calmer. A theme of aggressive families is lack of control (a "Take this job and shove it" attitude), which generally has been attributed to "being born this way." But with the skills they develop, family members discover they have more control both within the family setting and in other locations as well.

Positive Imagery

Families with conduct- or oppositional-defiant-disordered children frequently develop very negative images of their families and their children. In studies examining beliefs about families, families with normal-functioning children have positive attributes and images of family members, but in aggressive families the attributes and images are negative.

As a step in developing positive imagery, we direct parents in images.

> *Therapist:*   Terri, you say that when you are at work and think about going home you see fighting, yelling, and kids not minding you. It seems the more you imagine that, the less you want to go home. Is that right?
>
> *Terri:*   Yes, I get depressed before I even head home, just thinking about the hassles coming ahead. And then when I do get home and I see Jimmy and Evan doing something that they shouldn't, and I start to yell at them, I just picture what will happen if I say anything to them — it'll be hell for awhile — and I just figure it isn't worth it.
>
> *Therapist:*   So just imagining them not minding, fighting and arguing, causes you to stop. What I'd like to do is see if you can replace that with a more positive picture. I know the picture won't be true right now, but it can come true, and what I want you to do is work toward making it come true. If you can't even picture your goal, you can't achieve it. Let's begin practicing picturing it now. What I'd like to do is have you describe how you'd like things to be.

As the client describes situations that are desired, the therapist assists by having the client, in this case Terri, close her eyes and picture the scene. The important point to move toward is not one of mastery of all problems or a fantasy world that can't occur; rather, attention is directed toward helping Terri imagine that she can handle situations that are not pleasant, that she can practice her calming responses even though the children are not minding. At this time the notion of self-talk in introduced.

> *Therapist:*   Terri, what I want you to do now is picture yourself telling Jimmy and Evan that they have to go to their room and clean it up. You expect some difficulty getting them to mind, but picture yourself giving good, clear statements: Go to your room now and pick up your things. When that is done, you may come out and watch television, but not until it is satisfactory and there is no more fussing. Then picture yourself staying calm, even though they begin to talk back, and see yourself practicing your relaxation response as they go off still muttering. Now picture yourself saying to yourself that it isn't exactly as you want things to be but that you are making progress, you are moving in the right direction, and small steps have been taken. Remind yourself that from small steps come big changes and that you are well on your way — that you don't need to have everything perfect right now, just moving in the right direction.

Positive Reframing

Following the practice of positive self-talk, there is a need to look at the positive reframing of situations for parents. Positive reframing means taking a situation that they perceive as very negative and trying to reidentify it (reframe it) as a positive situation or at least a situation with the potential for a positive solution.

> *Therapist:* Terri, you say that the talking back and not minding drive you up the wall and that you can't stand to have the school on your back. Yet that isn't the worst situation I've ever heard of. Is it the worst you know of?
>
> *Terri* Well, no, I suppose they could be doing crazy occult stuff or be into weird sex stuff. But that doesn't mean I like what they are doing!
>
> *Therapist* Of course not, but let's look at it in a slightly different light. One of the functions of children is to grow away from their parents — after all, you don't want to have little children forever, but rather you want them to develop into young adults. One step in being a young adolescent is to move toward independence from one's parents — you did it, all adolescents move toward independence. Some times the move is smooth and there is little rebellion. Other times it is rockier. Although you don't like everything Jimmy and Evan are doing, at least you do admire them for moving toward autonomy, independence. Right?
>
> *Terri:* Well, yes, but I wish to hell they would do it in a different way!
>
> *Therapist:* Right. And that's what we're working on, helping them continue their very positive move toward independence and autonomy, but to learn more effective ways of doing it. You need to practice seeing what they are doing as a positive direction, just a poor choice of how to do it, and they use poor choices because they don't know any better. That's where parents and counselors come in — helping kids learn more effective ways of doing what is a natural thing for them to do.

Examining Irrational Beliefs

Tied to positive reframing is examining the beliefs that parents have. Parents use negative labels with their children, which leads to negative feelings toward them. We work with the family to identify thoughts that are likely to lead to angry or despondent feelings and look for opposing thoughts that may lead to more effective responding using the following format:

1. A situation occurs
2. The person has thoughts about the situation
3. The person feels consistently with what is being thought — angry thoughts lead to angry feelings
4. People behave consistently with how they feel
5. There are consequences for the behavior, which leads to a continuation of the cycle.

Therapist: Terri, it seems situations occur and you find yourself getting really upset about them — you don't seem to know what to do. Let's back up a little and examine the situation. Earlier, you gave an example of coming home and finding the two boys fighting. You immediately got angry and spanked both of them, which led to them getting really upset with you, and the cycle continued. It seems that when you came home and saw what was happening, you thought to yourself, Those boys know I can't stand this, and they do this just to upset me — they are bad and hateful. When you think thoughts like that, you get upset, rightly so because you are feeling consistently with what you are thinking, but what you are thinking is causing you to get upset and then do things you later regret. Let's take a closer look at the thoughts. First, you indicate that you can't stand the situation, but in fact you have stood it for several years and you are still standing it okay, so that is probably not a very productive thought to have. It just isn't accurate, but thinking it does make you feel discouraged, which isn't helpful. The second part of the thought is that they are fighting just to upset you. I doubt that's exactly true. They probably are fighting for a number of reasons, but you don't like it. And when you think they are bad, you also attribute to them an intention or a way of being that I'm not certain is accurate. Let's look at it differently. Let's say they are fighting because they have learned to do so for several reasons (there is a payoff in that Mom pays attention, they may get their way with whatever they were fighting about, they don't know how to handle problem solving and this is the only response pattern they have), and they aren't bad, but they do behave in ways you wish they wouldn't.

Now let's try examining this differently. You come home and the boys are fighting. Think to yourself, I don't like what they are doing but I can handle it . . . that's why I'm going to counseling, to learn better ways to handle this. Besides, they aren't bad, they are just behaving in a way they learned to behave, and they really don't know better ways to handle conflicts — that's part of my job as a parent, to teach them more effective ways of dealing with problems. And I can do it, but first I have to send them to their rooms so they can stop the cycle, and I need to give myself a couple minutes to practice my calming exercises. Then I can tackle the situation more effectively.

As noted earlier in identifying relationship-building skills (see Chapter 5), it is important to identify the situation, thoughts, feelings, and consequences related to the situation as the parents present the concerns that brought them to counseling. Because the therapist has been attending to each of the interlocking components throughout the sessions, by the time the teaching of self-control skills comes around there should be a wealth of examples and ideas that he or she can use with the family.

The therapist, in working with the family on self-control skills, must be able to pull together the individual components to help them understand the interconnectedness of various parts of self-control.

Therapist: We have reviewed the steps involved in learning effective self-control. They include developing proficiency in

- Positive problem solving
- Relaxation or calming responses
- Positive imagery
- Positive reframing
- Attacking nonproductive thinking patterns.

And these all go together. When you see a situation occur, you need to say, What's my goal? and define it as a way of getting the family to function more effectively, including getting the kids to mind. The second step is asking, What am I doing? and if the answer is getting upset or angry or depressed, then go to the next question, Is what I'm doing helping me to achieve my goal? And if the answer is no, then the next question is, What can I do differently? and the answer is relax, develop some positive image of how you would like things to work out, reframe the situation in a way that is more positive, and address any irrational or nonproductive thinking that prevents you from moving in the direction you need to be going.

It is quite important that these steps be practiced and discussed in detail, because the process is not one with which most parents are familiar. And even when family members indicate they understand, you can be fairly certain that time is needed to practice and rehearse the steps in a supportive and understanding situation.

SELF-CONTROL SKILLS FOR CHILDREN AND ADOLESCENTS

A variety of methods for helping young children learn self-control skills have been developed for both school and family use and for individual as well as group applications (Bolstad & Johnson, 1972; Camp, Blom, & van Doorninck, 1977; Kendall & Braswell, 1985; Kendall & Hollon, 1979; Kirby & Grimley, 1986).

The turtle technique is a specific self-control program designed to help children learn effective management of their behavior. The method, developed by Schneider and Robin (1976) for use in a classroom setting with emotionally disturbed children, has been adapted for use within the family setting to help antisocial children master the ability to slow themselves down and gain control over their actions. The process, as adapted for use with families with antisocial children, involves four steps.

1. Learning to respond to the cue word, "turtle." The child is taught that when the cue word is used, he or she is to "act like a turtle,"

which involves closing the eyes and pulling the arms and legs close to the body, just as a turtle pulls into its shell.

2. Relaxing while in the turtle position. The child is taught a muscle-tensing, muscle-releasing process in which he or she is instructed to tense the large muscle groups and then release the tension from all the muscles. Other methods of relaxation may be presented, but this approach has been well received by children.

3. Alternative solutions. The child is taught to identify the area of conflict, the problem situation, which causes them to be upset or act out in an aggressive manner. At this point the therapist must guide the situation, as children often have difficulty identifying situations in which they become out of control. Parents are requested to help the child carry out the process at home, and thus a version of the problem-solving steps they have been taught may be used with the child. This procedure includes having children learn the four steps of problem solving:

- What's my goal?
- What am I doing?
- Is what I'm doing helping me achieve my goal?
- What can I do differently?

4. Applying the steps. The child must learn to apply the steps in the home setting, typically using cues from the parents. Parents are to provide positive consequences for the child's successful use of the turtle cue-and-response pattern. Parents learn to correct the child if the applications are not completed properly.

Fleischman, Horne, and Arthur (1983) have developed a script to be used with aggressive children in a family treatment format:

So, sometimes mom and dad may tell you to do something and when you don't do it, they begin to get angry. When this happens, you start to get mad because you think they are picking on you. A good thing to remember at those times is how a turtle handles conflict. Do you know how a turtle behaves when it gets in trouble? It pulls into its shell, doesn't it? Let me tell you about one turtle that used to get in trouble a lot. His name was Timmy, Timmy the Turtle.

Timmy used to do things around the house, and sometimes those things were OK and he and his mom and dad got along just fine. But sometimes Timmy would forget to do the things his parents wanted, and they would get upset with him and start fussing. That would upset Timmy, and he'd get mad and start fussing back, and pretty soon the house would be full of fussing turtles. You just can't imagine how noisy that would be!

Well, one day Timmy was told to pick up his toys before he could play outside. Well, Timmy forgot . . . you know how turtles can forget sometimes. And he started playing with a friend. Then he heard his mom calling him, and he decided he'd run away because he didn't want to be fussed at again. So he ran away, or at least as fast as turtles can run, which of course isn't very fast.

As he lumbered down the road, he came across Old Mr. Tortoise, the wisest turtle in the area. Mr. Tortoise saw Timmy and asked him why he looked so sad. Timmy told Mr. Tortoise what had happened, and explained that sometimes he would just get so mad that he didn't know what to do. Then Timmy would start yelling at his parents and get in really bad trouble.

Mr. Tortoise smiled and said that he could understand that, because a long time ago, before he became so wise, he also would get upset and angry and just blurt out things that would get him in trouble. Timmy was surprised about this and asked him how he learned not to do that. Mr. Tortoise said, "Well, Timmy, I just learned to use my natural protection. . . my shell." Mr. Tortoise went on to tell Timmy that the way he handled conflicts was to pull into his shell, breathe deep and relax . . . calm down a little. Then he would think about the predicament he was in and decide how he would handle it. He would come up with about four or five ideas then figure out what would happen if he did each one of those things. Finally he would choose the best one for him and act on it. That's how he got to be so wise.

Well, Timmy was really excited about that idea. So he ran, as fast as turtles can run, back home; and when he got there he heard his mom calling out in an angry voice. Timmy went to her and told her he was sorry for running away, but he had talked with Mr. Tortoise and Mr. Tortoise had told him how to handle things better. He said "Watch!" and he pulled into his shell, relaxed, and came out smiling. Then he picked up the toys like he was told to do earlier. Timmy kept practicing pulling into his shell, relaxing, and considering a plan on how to handle things until he got really good at it. Then he and his mom and dad stopped getting so upset. In fact, his mom and dad started practicing doing the same things when they got upset because they knew that if Mr. Tortoise had told Timmy about it, it must be good. And they all got a lot happier living together.

Well, what do you think . . does that sound like something you could use? I have a feeling it is, so what I'd like to do now is have us practice it, practice being like turtles. (pp. 246–247)

The turtle technique works particularly well with younger children, but as children approach adolescence they are less inclined to engage in the exercise and so other approaches are necessary. Direct discussion of power or control has proven more effective than using the turtle technique. For example, with the Faux family, the turtle technique proved to be effective for helping Jimmy (age 11) and Evan (age 9) develop self-control skills at home. With the older sister, Cara (age 16), a more direct approach was used.

Therapist: Cara, you have talked about how angry and upset you become with your mother and with Jake and how you argue with them and with Jimmy and Evan. You even do some pretty dumb things as a result of your anger toward your family — like getting in fist fights with the boys and even with your mother. You've also hurt yourself a few times.

Cara: Yes, but I can't let them push me around. They don't have any right to be telling me what to do.

Therapist: Is what you're doing, the fighting, getting you what you want out of life?

Cara: No, but I can't let them push me around.

Therapist: My opinion is that what is happening is just what you don't want — by entering into fights and arguments with them, you are letting them control you. You are, in fact, giving in to their game; they pull your string and get you going. You don't know how to handle problems without fighting.

Cara: Sure I do, it's just that I can't let them get on my case all the time.

Therapist: Let's talk about what other options exist.

Our experience is that antisocial children and adolescents are not very good at generating alternatives. They do not know how to deal with power struggles in nonaggressive methods. When alternative solutions are developed for them, including stepping out of the conflict, practicing calming responses, and identifying effective solutions to problems, they report being able to do all of these things but that they will not work. Aggressive children and adolescents demonstrate a "macho bravado" and report that they can perform any of the skills necessary for effective problem management, but that the system (viz., the family, the teacher, their boss) will not be receptive to their efforts. When the child or adolescent is requested to demonstrate the skill, however, it is clear that they are unable to perform the behavior in an effective manner.

The therapist should be prepared for excuses about how the skills will not work and that the environment will prevent them from being successful. Encouraging the child to take the "as if" position for awhile during the session helps address the skills:

Therapist: Cara, what I'd like is for you to act as if the methods will work. What I mean is, I know you don't believe the methods will work, and they won't as long as you refuse to practice them, to try them. But they have worked with lots of other folks who sincerely wanted to be in charge of their lives instead of letting others take control of them. So try the behaviors a couple of times and act as if they will work. The good part about this exercise is that you can practice it for awhile, and if you don't like the way it feels after you've done it a few times, you can always continue doing what you used to do. Okay?

At this point, videotaping equipment is particularly useful. Working with children on video allows them to see that they are not able to effectively utilize the skills they reported they had. With videotaped excercises a child can practice a new skill and develop mastery; concurrently, the therapist is able to present the self-control strategies as a way of demonstrating control over a situation rather than having the situation control the child.

A complaint frequently expressed by clients is that the new skills do not "feel right." This feeling results from the fact that the skills are new and people tend not to be comfortable with new behaviors, regardless of whether the skill is learning a new tennis swing, playing a musical instrument, or assertively responding to parents and teachers:

> *Therapist:* Sure, Cara, it will feel uncomfortable to do these things the first few times. That's understandable. But let me ask you, do you know which side of the highway people in England drive on? They drive on the left side, just the opposite from us. When I visited England, I felt very uncomfortable driving on the left side — my gut kept telling me I was on the wrong side of the road. But what would have happened if I'd listened to my gut and driven on the right side of the road the way we do in America? Right, a crash or a wreck. Instead, even though it felt very uncomfortable, I had to follow my head, not my gut, and think about what I should do even if it didn't feel right. That's what I'm asking you to do now, to follow your head, because you know that these self-control skills will put you in charge of your life, whereas following your gut reaction keeps getting you in trouble.

Children can be instructed in the use of other self-control skills depending on their cognitive abilities. Relaxation training, thought stopping, replacing upsetting thoughts with calming thoughts, and self-selected time-out are methods older children seem to adapt to and utilize effectively. The clinician should remember that the ultimate goal of teaching the client more effective self-control skills is to improve communication within the family system. When individuals are angry or frustrated, they tend to communicate based on these emotions by yelling, lecturing, threatening, and so on. An individual who is calm and relaxed becomes a more effective communicator by sending clear and understandable messages to others.

Chapter 8
Establishing and Maintaining Effective Disciplinary Methods

Many families with an oppositional-defiant- or conduct-disordered child want to begin family therapy immediately with disciplinary methods for their children. We have found that by introducing components of managing the self and the environment first, family relationships begin improving quickly, so much so that by the time we introduce discipline nearly 50% of the concerns specified on the Goal Setting Form are no longer problems. Approximately half of the areas of complaint are handled by effective commands, structured interactions, and self-control skills. The goal of any disciplinary method is to effectively stop the antisocial behavior; it is preferable to prevent a problem from beginning rather intervening later with a punishment approach. For problems that have not been prevented through effective environmental interventions or self-control skills, effective disciplinary approaches are necessary.

It is important that disciplinary methods "fit the crime." There is no one standard disciplinary method used; rather, as the family describes the problems encountered, an attempt is made to tailor the intervention to fit the problem. Standard interventions include the following methods.

IGNORING

Ignoring the behavior of a child that is attention-getting and non-threatening is an effective way of extinguishing such behaviors. Ignoring is particularly useful for such child behaviors as whining, nagging, telling on other children, complaining, pouting, and acting bored.

Many children have conditioned their parents to respond to them by engaging in activities that are difficult to ignore. Prime times for children to engage in aggravating activities are when parents are talking on the telephone, reading the evening paper, watching television, preparing dinner, or entertaining others. Parents must learn to ignore the aggravating behavior, not attend to it, in order to provide an unsatisfactory experience for the child. The difficulty in using ignoring is that if children have previously learned to use the behavior to get attention, they will expect to continue being successful and will continue to use the approach, even when it does not appear to work. In fact, most children will escalate their attention-seeking attempts by engaging in even more nuisance behaviors, expecting the parents to succumb to the distractions.

Parents who are unable to ignore annoying behavior are not good candidates for this. Parents who practice ignoring for a few minutes and then decide that the method will not work, thereby reinforcing the child for continued nuisance behavior, teach the child to continue the acting-out behavior or even escalate it sooner to a higher level of distraction.

When parents are able to use ignoring effectively, they should continue with their activities while the child engages in the distracting behavior, but when the child ceases the behavior, the parents should, within a few minutes, express appreciation for how he or she is now behaving. It is important to teach parents to "catch the child being good" rather than always trying to catch her or him being bad.

The therapist should review with the parents the specific situations in which ignoring will be used in order to be certain that the application will be appropriate. It should not be used, for example, with such life-endangering behaviors as fire setting, running away, or damaging property. In these situations, more intensive interventions are required. It should also be noted that ignoring will work only if the parents have a reinforcing potential. Parents who have little interaction with their child are not likely to impact the child's behavior by ignoring because that represents the current level of interaction.

Although ignoring seems to be a fairly mild form of discipline and appears to be a noninvasive disciplinary method, some people take considerable exception to using the method because it also implies withholding love, care, and attention. If children equate attention with love and do not receive attention, they may assume they are unloved. Obviously, love is not an appropriate contingent factor for children. If this situation is encountered, more energy should be spent on helping parents find ways to increase appropriate behaviors (catch the child being good) and decrease the emphasis on ignoring. Therapists should be aware, though, that it is possible to increase positive, prosocial behaviors without decreasing negative, antisocial behaviors (Patterson, 1982).

If the goal is to both *increase* prosocial behavior and *decrease* antisocial behaviors, a combination of attending and ignoring is appropriate.

In summary, when making a determination to use ignoring as a disciplinary method, parents should follow these guidelines (Silberman & Wheelan, 1980):

1. If the behavior is ignored, can tangible, harmful consequences occur before it is sufficiently extinguished?
2. Does your way of ignoring communicate indifference or disapproval?
3. Is your attention important enough to the child that ignoring will make a difference? (p. 98)

GRANDMA'S LAW

Premack's principle (Premack, 1959), or "grandma's law," so named because most grandmothers know how to effectively use the approach regardless of the amount of psychology training they have had, is very useful in getting a child to engage in desired behaviors. By establishing a contingency plan in which the child must successfully complete a desired or expected activity before doing something he or she would prefer to do, children develop an awareness of what behaviors are expected of them and the rules instituted by parents. Children may be less likely to eat peas than to eat chocolate cake. Therefore, making the eating of chocolate cake contingent on successfully eating peas is likely to result in pea eating. Other examples include:

- Cut the grass, and then you may play ball.
- Wash the dishes, and then you may watch television.
- Do your homework, and then you may visit your friend.
- Straighten your room, and then you may go out.

Most parents who enter therapy know about grandma's law, but when asked how they apply the procedure, most of them seem to have it backward. They frequently present it as such:

- Okay, play ball for awhile, but then you have to cut the grass.
- Okay, watch television for awhile, but then you have to wash the dishes.
- Well, visit with your friend for awhile, but then you have to do your homework.
- Go out and play for awhile, but when you come back you must straighten your room.

Grandma's law is an approach that requires parents to present a situation and then be firm in their commitment to follow through. Because antisocial children have a history of expecting to get their way and avoiding responsibility, it is important for parents to apply the approach in a firm but caring manner, while maintaining consistency between parents and from one time to the next. Some parents report feeling cruel or guilty because they deprive their child of a desired activity, such as dessert after dinner, and it is essential to discuss these situations with parents. Parents who feel guilty about their disciplinary methods are not likely to effectively implement the techniques, and treatment should refocus on the parents' concerns at this point. Many parents think, I want my children to love me and if I don't let them have their way, they may not love me any more. Our experience in interviewing hundreds of children with conduct and oppositional defiant disorders is just the opposite — most of these children seek more limits for their behavior. These children want their parents to establish consistent, appropriate guidelines for their behavior, with reasonable consequences for disobeying.

Grandma's law works only if the family employs the procedure appropriately. Parents who require a child to eat vegetables before having dessert but allow a child who does not eat vegetables to slip into the kitchen after dinner for pie, will be ineffective in using this approach.

NATURAL AND LOGICAL CONSEQUENCES

Natural consequences are results that would happen naturally without adult intervention (e.g., not wearing a warm coat in the winter results in becoming cold; playing with an irritable cat may result in being scratched).

Logical consequences are results that occur when a rule or guideline is violated (e.g., not doing homework results in failing the assignment; staying out too late playing results in no television for the evening).

Natural and logical consequences are particularly useful for families with children who are irresponsible. The procedure involves having children experience a consequence of their behavior. A child who oversleeps but experiences no consequence of the act isn't likely to learn to be more responsible in the future — there is no learning from the experience.

One family we worked with complained of a son, Todd, who was 8 years old but still had to be awakened each morning, have his breakfast fixed and his clothes laid out, and at times even had to be assisted in getting dressed. The mother hated mornings because she was constantly complaining and reminding Todd he had to get moving or he would miss the bus. Todd was able to get up and get dressed and eat

on weekend mornings without constant reminders from Mom. The program we developed was to instruct Todd that he would have an alarm
clock to awaken him, he was to select his clothes and get dressed, and
he was to fix his own breakfast. He was told that if he didn't do these
things, then he would be put out in front of the house when the bus
came and would have to go to school as he was, pajamas and all.

The next morning Todd followed his usual routine and wasn't ready
when the bus came. As promised, Mom put him out on the front steps
with his clothes in a bag and told him to catch the bus in his pajamas.
Not being completely without wits, Todd ran behind the house and
hid, as we had expected he might do. Mom found him and put him in
the car and told him, "Okay, today only I will drive you to school.
When we get there I am putting you out in front of the school regardless
of whether you are dressed or not." Todd was dressed by the time they
reached the school, and the next morning he managed to get himself
out of bed, dressed, and ready for the bus. Logical consequences of
one's behavior do indeed pay off in parenting.

TIME-OUT

Time-out, which is an extension of logical consequences, involves
isolating the child for a few minutes following an instance of misbehavior. This procedure is particularly useful for noncompliance, defiance,
and other instances in which immediate cessation of the interaction is
important. Time-out is not used as a way of "getting even" with the
child for misbehaving; rather, it is seen as a means of stopping the
aversive interaction from continuing, or of eliciting compliance. Time-
out, as the name implies, provides a time out from the interaction so
that the child can calm down, relax, review the alternatives available,
and then reenter the family interaction in a more positive way.

Time-out involves having the parents remove the child from the situation for a brief period (usually about 5 minutes). Often the bathroom
or a laundry room is used as the time-out room, although other locations
may be used as well. The time-out location should be one where the
child receives little stimulation, for the purpose of the procedure is to
allow him or her time to review the situation and calm down, not to
become interested in other activities. The child's room, which may have
toys or other distracting items, is not generally an appropriate location
for time-out. Likewise, a chair in the corner of a living room or kitchen
is typically not a good location for time-out because the child is usually
able to obtain attention while in these rooms. If a child is highly aggressive, the selected location should be "child-proofed" by making
certain that any items that can hurt the child or that can be used by the

child to destroy the room are removed. When disciplinary action is needed outside the home, other locations for time-out may be necessary; for example, a park bench, a car (if it is safe), or other places that allow the child an opportunity to calm down can be used.

A concern parents frequently present is what to do if the child refuses to go to time-out. We have encountered very little difficulty with this issue because of the way the procedure is presented to the child:

Therapist: Jimmy and Evan, we have talked a little about time-out today. What do you think about this technique?

Evan: I don't know.

Jimmy: I don't like it. I don't want to have to go and sit in the stupid bathroom.

Therapist: I understand that. And I agree, it doesn't sound like much fun. However, let's look at it another way. Do you remember a few weeks ago when we first met and I asked you to tell me how you would like your family to be different, how you would like it to change? You told me then that you wanted your mom to quit yelling at you and spanking you. You also said Jake was on your case, yelling at you a lot, and that you wanted him to stop. Remember? Well, what I'm proposing is that time-out be used as a way to get both your mom and Jake to quit yelling at you and to use time-out rather than spankings. How does that sound?

As a further contribution to the success of the approach, it is important that time-out be practiced in the session several times under different circumstances (e.g., with the therapist demonstrating the method, the parents carrying it out, the children cooperating as well as resisting). The therapist should be certain that the parents know how to apply the procedure and have selected an appropriate setting for its use. Parents must also understand that time-out is not for revenge but to establish a cooling-off period which increases cooperation. Even with careful preparation, we have had more difficulty with parents understanding time-out than any other method. We have had a number of parents who insist that time-out should be lengthy (e.g., an hour to a day in length), that it should be punishing (e.g., lock the child in a basement or closet), or that it needs additional consequences (e.g., spank the child before placing him or her in time-out).

EXTRA CHORES

There are times when the above disciplinary methods are not effective. Lying, for example, is not impacted by time-out or grandma's law, nor are such behaviors as damaging property or stealing likely to change with the less invasive disciplinary approaches. Assigning extra chores or work often has a powerful impact on aggressive children. As with other disciplinary methods, the punishment should fit the crime, which means that some behaviors may have a small chore assigned (e.g., fibbing may result in extra bathroom cleaning assignments), and other behaviors may result in extensive tasks (e.g., stealing a large item may result in having to tend a garden or weed the entire yard in addition to making restitution to the victim).

There are some considerations parents should review when assigning extra chores. One involves what the chore entails — is it time or task? For example, if weeding a section of garden is assigned, is the child assigned a time period (for 1 hour?) or a space (a 6-foot square?). Because aggressive children are unlikely to leap at the opportunity to complete a chore, it is usually best to make assignments based on the task. A second consideration is the quality of the work. Before using extra chores parents should discuss with the child what it means to do the job in an acceptable manner so that he or she knows what is expected. A third consideration is the scope of the assignment. We usually ask parents to review the assignment with us before its implementation because parents often give chores when they are angry, which may result in job assignments that are too harsh. The therapist can often help in developing reasonable expectations.

LOSS OF PRIVILEGES

The final disciplinary method is loss of privileges. This procedure is presented last because it is one that can be implemented when all others fail. There are situations that do not respond well to other approaches. If a child refuses to comply with a parental command, for example, other disciplinary methods may not be adequate. If the child refuses to go into time-out and extra chores are refused, the parents must provide a consequence; thus one of the few approaches left is the loss of a privilege.

Each child differs in what she or he considers important privileges, but the therapist, in cooperation with the parents, should be able to identify several appropriate selections. The privilege may be having dessert, riding a bicycle, watching television, playing with friends, going to a sporting event or movie, or some other similar activity. Parents must understand that they should not initiate discipline with this method, as it often leads to arguments and power struggles and can become ineffective if used too extensively. When children have no privileges left to lose, they can act with impunity.

Problems that develop when using this approach include parents using an excessive privilege loss (You can't play outside for 3 weeks), repeating themselves (You lost an hour of television earlier, now you lose another hour of it), and failure to immediately revoke the privilege (You can't go to Bill's party next month). It is also inappropriate to revoke an earned privilege (I know you worked cutting grass all summer to earn the money to buy a radio, but now you can't buy one because of what you did).

IMPLEMENTATION CONSIDERATIONS

In implementing disciplinary approaches, therapists must attend to several considerations for the program to work as effectively as possible.

In-session Rehearsal

Most families will indicate they are familiar with the disciplinary methods presented. This does not mean, however, that they understand the methods or that they are adept at using them. Most parents who enter therapy are not effective in their discipline; otherwise they would not be involved in therapy. The therapist must provide a rationale for each method presented, including stating why the particular approach is appropriate for addressing the behaviors presented as problems by a family and the reasons it should be effective with a child.

Beyond a simple explanation of the disciplinary method, the therapist should demonstrate, through modeling, how to use the technique with the child. After demonstrating several ways to use the technique, the therapist should have the parents practice the technique while she or he role-plays being the child. After the parents have had an opportunity to practice with the therapist as the child, they should then practice the method in a role-play format with their children, first with the children being cooperative in the role play and then with the children being uncooperative.

Anticipating Problems

After selecting a disciplinary approach, explaining its use, and practicing the method, the therapist should discuss what may go wrong once the family leaves the therapy room.

> *Therapist:* Okay, it seems that you understand how to use grandma's law, time-out, and loss of privileges. Now what I'd like for you to do is picture that you have left here and it is tomorrow night. You start to use the methods we've talked about tonight. Tell me, what do you think could go wrong? What could cause the methods to not work?

> *Lynne:* Well, if we are over at Jake's family's house and we have to use this stuff, they'll just laugh at us and tell us it is stupid to be going to a counselor. I don't think we could use it around them.
> *Therapist:* A good example. Now, let's talk about how to handle that situation.

At this point the therapist can spend time with the family exploring ways to handle all the problems presented, for if the parents experience problems and have not figured out how to handle them in advance, they are likely to stop trying to use the disciplinary method.

Another step the therapist may take to ensure implementation of the selected disciplinary approaches is to schedule telephone calls to the family to learn how the process is going.

> *Therapist:* Jake and Lynne, what I'd like to do is call you in, let's say, two nights and see how time-out is going. That way if you are having any problems that we haven't anticipated, then you don't have to wait a whole week to come in and talk about them. . . .I really don't want us to lose a week when we could be using the time. So tell me, when is a good time to call you in two or three nights?

Most family members are leery, at least initially, of receiving weekly telephone calls from their therapist to check on their use of disciplinary procedures. Parents will frequently report not having had an opportunity to employ the method or that the child did not comply when the discipline was attempted. It is not assumed that the parents are resistant to the use of the discipline approach, but that they simply may not fully understand its application or actually have not had an opportunity to employ it. At this point, we have found it useful to ask the parents to role-play the disciplinary approach while the therapist listens over the phone. If the child is not available, the therapist simply asks the parents, "If I call back in two hours will you have had an opportunity to use time-out?" Typically, the parent will reply affirmatively, and the therapist will make a call to the family after the specified length of time. On completion of treatment, many families have described the weekly telephone calls as one of the most appreciated and encouraging experiences.

Addressing Children's Concerns

The therapist should spend time with the children during this phase of the treatment to identify concerns they may have about the family treatment program. The therapist must not be seen as simply a parent ally — working with the parents against the children. Rather, the children should understand that their concerns are also important and that the therapist has not forgotten the goals established when initial contacts with the children occurred.

The therapist must also attend to issues of fairness and equality at this time. It may appear to the children that they are being required to do all the changing and that the parents are being treated preferentially. To address the issue of fairness, the therapist can ask the children to track their parents' behavior and to assist the entire family in keeping records on whether the disciplinary methods are being applied properly (e.g., Did Mom send you to time-out without yelling, as we agreed?).

Predict Problems

The therapist will be able to anticipate potential problems during the week when new discipline approaches are implemented, and it is important to predict that these problems are likely to occur. If such problems do indeed occur, the parents will probably attribute understanding and expertise to the therapist for being aware of what would happen. Should the problems not develop, the parents will usually construe this to mean the program is working very well, or the family may forget the predictions or tease the therapist about being off on the forecast.

> *Therapist:* Now Lynne, one thing I will predict is that this week Jimmy and Evan are likely to increase their acting-out rather than decrease it. I know that sounds crazy with you beginning a disciplinary program designed to reduce the acting-out, but what happens is that the kids begin to really test you, to see if you mean it when you tell them you are going to consistently use the new techniques — they'll test you to see if you really are going to use the skills and be consistent. So look for an increase in misbehavior, not a decrease.

In our clinical experience, we have found this system of checks and balances (viz., making sure the disciplinary method is understood and employed correctly while encouraging and reinforcing its utilization by parents) to work effectively in teaching disciplinary methods to parents. This also implies that the therapist has sufficient knowledge of the discipline procedures to be aware of and to predict potential problems associated with their use.

Chapter 9
Establishing and Maintaining Effective Family Interactions

The disciplinary methods described in chapter 8 are designed to reduce antisocial behaviors. Additionally, it is essential to increase prosocial behaviors, as families not only want to reduce friction, they also want to increase the pleasure of being in a family. All steps in the treatment to this point have contributed to increasing prosocial behaviors. Everyone in the family enjoys each other's company more and behaves more pleasantly when clear expectations are established, parent requests are fair and delivered in a respectful manner, family members are calm and relaxed as they deal with each other, and aversive behavior is reduced.

Families with a history of conduct- or oppositional-defiant-disordered behavior on the part of their children need to specifically address the issue of increasing positive interactions. Aggressive children generally do not respond well to positive approaches until they have experienced the changes family members make during the earlier stages of the treatment program. By this point in the treatment even highly aggressive children have learned that therapy works to create a family environment that is respectful, fair, and moving toward an environment in which all family members experience being treated with consideration and dignity. To increase prosocial behaviors, two types of reinforcement are presented, formal reward systems and social interaction.

FORMAL REWARD SYSTEMS

Three formal systems have been developed for establishing prosocial behaviors: point systems, allowances, and contracting. These are discussed in the following sections and in more detail in Fleischman, Horne, and Arthur (1983).

Point Systems

Point systems involve identifying desired behaviors and providing some form of reward system for engaging in those behaviors. Points are tallied on a daily tally sheet and, at a designated time (the end of the week, usually), the child is allowed to receive a special privilege or treat. The point system may be somewhat casual, with parents passing out tokens (poker chips or other designated objects) and collecting them at a given time in exchange for the privilege, or the system may be more formalized with the family using a printed checklist with spaces for marking points or applying stickers such as smiling faces or stars.

Point systems work most effectively with younger children, with families in which parents have somewhat regular schedules so that they can consistently provide points, and in families that can specify behaviors clearly enough to assign points for the system. Our experience suggests that point systems are more effective and less conflictual with low-income families, as extra money for allowances is often not available. Children in such families may "cash in" their points for particular activities that do not require extra financial support (e.g., camping in the living room, having friends over to watch a TV movie).

Allowances

Allowances work well with older children and allow parents to tie a financial payment to chores or tasks to be completed. Money is a strong motivator for older children and, although it still represents a type of point system, it can be tied more to tasks accomplished than to the social activities often used in point systems. When initiating an allowance system, sufficient money should be available to provide a daily payment; once the program is underway and working, parents may move to more extended payment periods.

Contracting

Contracting provides a process whereby family members agree to work cooperatively to accomplish tasks. One person specifies an activity or task they would like the other to complete and also specifies what that individual will receive in return.

- If you finish your homework by 7, you may watch television until 8:30.
- If your room is picked up by 3:30, I'll play a game with you.

Contracting works effectively with older children and is a procedure that may be used if there are insufficient funds for an allowance or if interactions with family members carry more reinforcement value than an allowance.

SOCIAL INTERACTIONS

During earlier sessions, parents have been taught to speak with their children in a caring manner, treat their children as nicely as they would a stranger or a neighbor, and be clear in their expectations. When discussing social interactions, the therapist continues to build on this earlier work.

Verbal Attending

Verbal interactions are presented as a positive way to increase prosocial behaviors. Most families with conduct or oppositional defiant disorders are expert at delivering critical statements, put-downs, and sarcastic remarks, but they do not know how to compliment, praise, or share positive feelings toward other family members. Gottman, Notarius, Gonso, and Markman (1976) found that 57% of the communication of nondistressed couples was positive, versus 37% for distressed couples, and Horne and Fuelle (1981) noted that compared with mothers of nonclinic-referred children, mothers of impulsive and socially aggressive children were more critical, had difficulty staying on a topic, and failed to resolve conflicts. We do not know whether distressed families communicate poorly because they are distressed, or whether they are distressed because they communicate poorly. We do know that as families participate in treatment and become less distressed, their communication patterns improve, partly because of direct intervention in communication styles.

The therapist needs to draw on previous interactions with the family to provide examples of times when the family has been too critical and may have been more positive. The therapist teaches parents the importance of building self-esteem and self-confidence through supportive and encouraging statements rather than attempting to tear down the child. In sessions the therapist rehearses with all family members ways of expressing care and understanding. For many parents there will be considerable discomfort in making positive statements, for they have not experienced family interactions in which positive support is the standard. In that case, it will be necessary to start with less threatening statements (e.g., I saw you playing nicely with your brother; I certainly like seeing that) and progressively build to more intense statements (e.g., I love you and appreciate the effort you are putting forth to help the family function better). As family members practice making positive statements to one another in therapy, they will become more comfortable using them at home.

Nonverbal Attending

As the research cited earlier by James (1987) indicates, there are no differences in the *amount* of touching that occurs in families with conduct-and oppositional-defiant-disordered children and families with children who are well-functioning. She does report, though, that there were considerable differences in *how* the family members touched. Families with aggressive children used more controlling and disciplinary touch, while functional families used touch to communicate in positive ways, including affection and support.

Families in therapy should be taught to touch in affectionate ways and to express caring and support through physical contact, rather than to use touch as a discipline or punishment. Many parents of aggressive children report feeling uncomfortable ("sissy") when touching. When talking about ways of touching, however, most family members admit to enjoying touch if it is socially sanctioned. Many men have even admitted to not liking the macho hitting and poking in which so many of them engage, although they are uncomfortable discussing this with their male friends. In providing a positive guideline for family touching, the therapist can give permission for family members to demonstrate their caring both verbally and physically.

A caveat to the encouragement of physical contact is to be certain that there is no confusion of sexual identity or sexual roles in the family system. With many of the families referred to our treatment program from Child Protective Services (CPS) and other social service agencies, therapists have had to work toward limiting physical contact when there have been concerns about sexual abuse. The history and potential for sexual or physical abuse should be carefully explored with these families.

Intent-Impact Model

Gottman et al. (1976) have described what they call an intent-impact model for teaching effective communication skills. Their target group was couples, but we have applied the concept to an entire family. Gottman et al. (1976) indicate that in a communication pattern there is a sender and a receiver:

A: Sends message   B: Receives message

Good communication is said to occur when B receives the message sent by A. Communication patterns have room for considerable interference, however. For example, A may intend to send the message: I like the way you straightened your room. Clear delivery of the message, though, may not occur if there is interference on the part of the sender. If A, for example, has a headache, had a bad day at work, is feeling stressed, or in some other way is not feeling well, a message that is well intended may come across as critical or as a put-down.

At the same time, the receiver, B, may have an interference operating. For example, if B had a bad day, or perhaps is feeling guilty about not doing some things around the house that had been requested, then B may hear the statement from A with interference and interpret the intent to be a put-down or a criticism. According to Gottman et al. (1976), effective communication occurs when the intent of A (viz., I like the way you straightened your room) has the impact intended (viz., He liked the way I straightened my room). Any time that does not happen, poor communication occurs.

In working with distressed families, it becomes clear that they usually do not know how to communicate in such a way that their intent and impact are consistent. Through practice and role plays in session, the therapist may help family members master these skills.

Effective Communication

Gordon (1970), in his book on parent-effectiveness training, described many communication skills that are helpful for family members to master in order to establish a "no-lose" relationship, one in which each member of the family may benefit and experience positive growth rather than be subjected to sarcasm, criticism, and put-downs.

Dinkmeyer and McKay (1982) suggested that effective communication between parent and child consists of three phases. First, exploring alternatives allows the parent and child to brainstorm possible solutions to problems and then evaluate their potential effectiveness. Second, defining problem ownership places the focus for decision making squarely on the shoulders of the individual with the problem by asking whose problem it is, who is experiencing difficulty with whom, and whose purposes are not being met. Third, utilizing "I" messages keeps parents and children from placing blame on someone else for their problem. When responding in anger, communication is stifled and children become "parent-deaf"; thus, effective communication between parent and child involves both listening and talking in a respectful and caring manner.

Fleischman et al. (1983) state that effective verbal communication should follow these guidelines:

1. Speak your piece.
2. Use "I" messages instead of "you" messages.
3. Be specific.
4. Be brief.
5. Check to see that others are listening.
6. Find out what others are thinking.
7. Show that you're listening.
8. Ask questions if you're confused.
9. Stop and let others know when communication is breaking down. (pp. 175–178)

Additionally, Fleischman et al. (1983) state that the following communication patterns should be avoided.

1. Put-downs
2. Blaming
3. Denial
4. Defensiveness
5. Communicating hopelessness
6. Mind reading
7. Talking for others
8. Sidetracking (pp. 179–181)

APPLYING FAMILY COMMUNICATION SKILLS

Daily Problem Solving

Parents are encouraged to identify a specific time each day when they will sit down as a family and use their communication skills to address current problems. One time that may be particularly appropriate is after dinner, when the kitchen has been straightened up and each person is moving toward other activities. The purpose of a daily problem-solving exercise is to have all members of the family together, using positive communication skills, to discuss topics of interest to them and address any problems that are occurring and need attention. It is not to be used as a daily "gripe session," but rather as a time to discuss both the positives and negatives of what has occurred during the day. A daily meeting provides a setting in which all family members can interact, listen to one another, and be listened to by the others. The primary purpose is to have each family member show attention to and caring for other members of the family.

Weekly Family Meetings

Dinkmeyer and McKay (1976) have described the Adlerian process of holding weekly family meetings. The purpose of these meetings is for the parents and children to plan family fun, resolve problems, share positive feelings, and plan for the distribution of household chores. We schedule weekly family meetings for similar purposes, but also just for the social occasion of being together at a scheduled time.

Daily problem-solving and weekly family meetings need to occur while the family is still in therapy, so the therapist can review with the family how the meetings progress. The therapist may want to use part of the therapy session to conduct a family problem-solving meeting for the purpose of observing and providing feedback on ways to improve the quality of the interactions.

IMPLEMENTING AND MAINTAINING CHANGE

Families with oppositional-defiant- or conduct-disordered children who engage in the methods presented up to this point generally experience positive change quickly. These positive changes may not continue to be maintained without attention to the details of working with families.

Defining and Monitoring the Problem

Early in treatment Goal Setting Forms were completed which defined the problems to be addressed in therapy. These goals must be clearly defined, measurable, and agreed on by the participating family members. Once treatment begins, the family will monitor progress toward achieving these goals, including daily recordings of progress on self-control, discipline, and positive interactions. The goals should be reviewed each week to determine the amount of progress being achieved and to identify whether additional goals need to be added in order to expand treatment efficacy. Parents should be cautioned to establish reasonable expectations for their children; our experience is that once parents begin having success with their change programs they continue to increase expectations and establish new goals. The therapist should monitor this situation to be certain that the expectations are reasonable. Further, the children involved should be included in the goal-setting and evaluation process to be certain that they are experiencing positive changes within the family as well. The purpose of treatment is to change family interactions in a positive direction, in essence, to change the family system. The purpose is not to teach parents skills for manipulating their child's behavior to the extent that they are the parents of an unhappy but conforming child.

An issue that develops after treatment begins is that parents realize the extent of effort and commitment they must put forth to bring about the desired changes in their family, including personal change for themselves. This concern may be addressed during the initial presentation of treatment but also must be attended to on a regular basis during treatment. Fortunately, when parents follow through with assignments, change on the part of their children occurs quickly and is reinforcing, but these changes alone may not sustain the parents without attention, support, and encouragement from the therapist. Continued participation in treatment by the parents cannot be assumed just because progress is occurring. A number of therapist activities seem helpful, including giving parents credit for the changes (e.g., You've really done a great job; you certainly seemed to be able to take the ball and run with it when it came to helping Billy become more compliant and cooperative around the house), defining cause-and-effect relationships rather than attributing behavior to noncontrollable phenomena (e.g., When we started, you seemed to feel Maria was just "born bad," but now you are able to identify when she's going to act up and you can take steps to prevent the problem. You are able to figure out the relationship between her behavior and the payoffs she gets for behaving the way she does). One of the most powerful impacts on parental participation seems to be telephone calls. Calling the family to find out how they are doing during the week provides encouragement to follow through in their assignments, which then leads to greater success. Telephone contacts appear to be a reinforcer for the family, indicating to them that the therapist cares enough to take the time to check on them. We have had families request that the phone calls continue even after therapy stops.

In-home Visitations

In addition to weekly telephone calls and meetings with school personnel, in-home visitations should be conducted on a regular basis (e.g., once per month or every fourth session). Our experience has been that most families appreciate not having the added expense of traveling to the clinic for their treatment session and like having an opportunity the show the therapist what they experience in their own households. Observations of the home environment also provide the therapist with a first-hand view of what it may be like to be part of the family and offers an opportunity to employ various treatment techniques in the setting within which they will be utilized. For example, the therapist may work with the family to prepare a time-out room or note other changes in the environment that could help family members be more effective in conducting their treatment assignments.

Consultation with Significant Others

On occasion it may be useful to consult with extended family members, religious figures, or agency personnel to ensure that the therapist is gaining a comprehensive view of family concerns. If family members are not following through with assignments because of certain religious commitments or doctrines, the therapist would be wise to consult with a religious leader of their client's faith to clarify the client's interpretation of these tenets. Most clients are open to inviting their priest, rabbi, preacher, or bishop to discuss issues with their therapist, and this consultation typically results in discussions of a client's misunderstanding of religious doctrine or strict adherence to behaviors which have no religious base but were learned from other family members (viz., parents, grandparents).

If the conduct- or oppositional-defiant-disordered child has been referred by the juvenile court system, it is likely that he or she will be participating in community service for restitution purposes. If this is the case, the therapist may need to contact the child's supervisor to determine what type of work is being done and whether the child is performing satisfactorily. It is possible that the child is not completing the necessary work and has learned that the system really is not providing any punishment; in fact, he or she may have been able to beat the system and get away with the crime. In this case, implementing and maintaining behavior change is undermined by failure to provide appropriate consequences.

Extended-family members can also have a major impact on implementing behavior change programs. When clients are not supported in their efforts by their loved ones, they may develop self-doubt and are less likely to complete treatment assignments. The therapist should make a thorough assessment of relationships between clients and extended family members to ensure cooperation and support, or at least to avoid discouragement.

Chapter 10

Extending the Change Program and Ensuring Maintenance

GOING BEYOND THE IMMEDIATE FAMILY

Initially treatment for families with conduct or oppositional defiant disorders begins in the home, simply because it is much more difficult for parents to manage children's behavior outside the home. Treatment begins with in-home problem areas, such as complying (minding), playing cooperatively with siblings, going to bed on time, and related activities. Once parents have achieved success with the initial areas of concern, the Goal Setting Form is revised to include problems outside the immediate household.

For Jimmy Faux, the Goal Setting Form initially included problems at home except for one area, school problems (see Figure 6.3). When the Faux family reviewed the goals for Jimmy, it was decided to initially attend to three areas, cooperation, minding, and his room, because all three could be identified as noncompliance issues and could be treated through a noncompliance program using the interventions described. Once Jimmy stopped fighting with Evan, reduced his arguing and talking back, kept his room clean, and complied well with requests made by family members, the goals were reviewed and additional areas of concern were identified. At this point it was agreed that Jimmy also demonstrated the following problem areas:

1. *Stealing.* Jimmy would come home with items he had "found" or that had been "given" to him. The items were small — pencils, note-

books, candy, toy cars — but the pattern was consistent, with Jimmy coming home with a questionable item at least once a week.

2. *Fighting.* Jimmy managed to get into arguments that generally led to fights with neighborhood boys at least twice a week. He always explained that the fights occurred because other boys picked on him and he had to defend himself.

3. *Neighborhood conflicts.* Several times a week neighbors called the mother, Terri, to report that Jimmy had been causing trouble in the neighborhood. Problems included throwing rocks at dogs and at buildings, breaking clotheslines, and using profanity with neighbors who told him to stop misbehaving.

4. *Inappropriate sexual activity.* Parents from two different families with girls reported to Terri that Jimmy had been using sexually explicit language around the girls and had asked them to engage in exhibitionary acts with him.

5. *School.* The school problems had continued, with Jimmy skipping school about once every other week, engaging in fights with others at school, talking back to the teacher, and experiencing poor academic performance.

A decision was made to continue to put school problems on hold while attending to the additional family problem areas. For problem areas 1 through 4, increased monitoring of Jimmy's whereabouts was instituted to increase his accountability for his time and location. This process included having him closely monitored by the grandmother, Lynne. Jimmy had to check in with Lynne at least every half hour and account for his whereabouts, which would occasionally be checked by Lynne through phone calls or walks through the neighborhood. If Jimmy had been behaving, he received points, and if he had been misbehaving (viz., fighting, in conflict with neighbors), he went home where he stayed the remainder of the day, and further, he was assigned a task or chore to complete.

In addition to attending to Jimmy's whereabouts, the therapist met with him and Evan to review ways of interacting positively with friends, attempting to generalize the communications skills learned within the family for application with peers. Finally, the therapist spent time with Jimmy discussing adolescent sexual issues, including appropriate and inappropriate expression of emerging sexuality.

For the stealing problem, a stealer program modeled on the work of Reid (Patterson, Reid, Jones & Conger, 1975; Reid & Hendricks, 1973; Reid & Patterson, 1976) was utilized. The program involves explaining to the child and the parents that stealing will not be tolerated. Stealing is operationally defined, with examples, and the explanation is given that if the child "finds" things or is "given" things, that will also count as stealing unless there is some verification of the gift (e.g., a note from a teacher saying he or she gave Jimmy a pencil for his good performance that day).

The stealing program involves providing restitution to the offended party if it is possible to identify her or him. This includes returning stolen toy cars to the store from which they were taken, apologizing, and paying for the stolen items. In addition to providing restitution, the stealer is required to complete a chore or task around the house in addition to his or her regular duties as payment for causing the parents trouble.

Because the earlier treatment methods for changing Jimmy's in-home behavior were effective, he learned that he could depend on the family being fair and equitable and that through counseling the family would work to resolve their problems. This increased his confidence that treatment interventions would lead to better family interactions and support in his efforts to change out-of-home behaviors from aggressive and inappropriate to responsible and age-appropriate.

Addressing School Problems

The majority of our referrals for treatment come from school sources, followed by Child Protective Services (CPS) and juvenile courts and churches. The minority of referrals come from families themselves, although once a family is in treatment we begin with family problems and changes within the home rather than attending immediately to outside issues such as school problems. Our experience has been that, whereas problems outside the home generally lead to the referral, family members are not able to begin instituting change outside the home until they have developed skills and had success in implementing change within the home structure. A family that cannot control a child's behavior at home cannot influence the child's behavior at school, but once the family has learned to effectively manage the child at home, these changes may generalize to the school setting. We do, however, contact the school and the child's teacher immediately to notify them that we are beginning work with the family and that after initial contacts with the family yield positive results, we will initiate a school program. Our previous work with teachers has resulted in cooperation and agreement to delay school intervention for a few weeks in order to develop family change and support first.

In establishing a school program the therapist should meet with school personnel involved with the child. Generally it is best to schedule a meeting that includes parents, school personnel, and the therapist to review problems at school and establish goals for change. The therapist can be very helpful in this context because teachers and parents frequently have developed an adversarial relationship resulting from the child's acting out at school and the family's failure to correct the behavior. The therapist is able to reframe the problem into a learning situation in which the parents learn more effective skills for managing their child, and the teacher learns of the circumstances that have previously prevented the family from being effective in their efforts with the child.

The therapist, in conjunction with the family and the teacher, develops a new Goal Setting Form specifically oriented toward school problems. The teacher identifies the changes that are expected, much along the lines of the goals established for the home but specifically oriented toward classroom and school topics. Based on the goals selected, the therapist, in conjunction with the teacher, develops a Daily Home Report Card which the teacher completes at the end of each day. The student takes the Daily Home Report Card to the parents so that they may provide the consequences — positive if the report card is favorable, negative if the report card indicates problems during the day. It is the student's responsibility to take the report card home each day, and failure to do so is considered a negative report, with the parents providing a consequence that is appropriate. A sample home report card for Jimmy is shown in Figure 10.1.

The therapist coordinates with the teachers what will be included on the Daily Home Report Card. The report should start with tasks that have a likelihood of being achieved, because it is better to have the student experience initial success in the school program so that success

	M		T		W		Th		F	
	Y	N	Y	N	Y	N	Y	N	Y	N
Attended school	___		___		___		___		___	
Turned in homework										
Spelling	___		___		___		___		___	
Social studies	___		___		___		___		___	
Math	___		___		___		___		___	
___	___		___		___		___		___	
___	___		___		___		___		___	
Cooperative in class	___		___		___		___		___	
Cooperative at recess	___		___		___		___		___	
Cooperative at lunch	___		___		___		___		___	

FIGURE 10.1. Daily Home Report Card.

becomes the foundation on which to build as additional steps are instituted. The therapist also works with the family and the student to identify what reasonable consequences will be, including providing rewards for appropriate work and chores or additional work for areas that are unsatisfactory. It is also the therapist's responsibility to help parents deal with areas that will be unclear, including topics such as what to do if a child brings home a report with some positives and some negatives. Are the positives rewarded and the negatives assigned extra chores? Most parents are not highly skilled in the problem-solving steps that will allow them to handle such conflicting situations.

When establishing the school program, teachers must realize that the Daily Home Report Card will not be too time-consuming. In fact, it is quite simple, requiring only 15 to 30 seconds to complete each day, and is dropped from use when the child's behavior approximates that of other children in the classroom.

The therapist also reviews with the teacher steps being taken by the parents to provide more appropriate interactions for the child's behavior in the home and then reviews with the teacher possible ways to institute a similar program within the classroom. There are teachers who will be highly receptive to assistance in this area, whereas others will assume that classroom activities are solely under the jurisdiction of the teacher and will not be receptive to suggestions from a therapist. We explore with the teacher possible uses of disciplinary methods for the entire class (e.g. ignoring, grandma's law, natural and logical consequences, time-out, loss of privileges). Our experience is that most teachers have been trained in such classroom disciplinary methods but that many have forgotten them or did not know how to effectively implement the techniques in their classrooms. When several children in a single school have been treated in our program, we have conducted in-service training for any teacher interested in reviewing the procedures.

See Fleischman, Horne, and Arthur (1983) for an extended discussion of ways to implement a school intervention program for aggressive, antisocial children.

Working With Agencies

Working with agencies involved in providing services for conduct- or oppositional-defiant-disordered children can be complex, confusing, and frustrating. Several areas of cooperation require attention, however, if coordination of services is to have optimal benefits for the children and their families.

Who Does What? Most people involved in working with youths do so because they want to help them and believe they are providing a useful service. This does not mean, though, that all human service personnel are therapists. When therapists are involved in working with children, either through referral or directly through the center's operation, there must be a clarification of who will provide therapy and who will be responsible for other services the child may receive. Duplication of services or inconsistencies in work may result if there is not a clear coordination of responsibilities. This is particularly important with aggressive, antisocial youth who quickly begin to attempt to play one helper against another, similar to the way in which they may have played one parent against the other.

We have encountered the need to clarify roles and responsibilities, particularly when working with CPS units or welfare department programs, because many caseworkers want to provide direct counseling services to their clientele. It is quite important that the services be coordinated and that a clear delineation of responsibilities be identified. Depending on the setting in which the treatment is being conducted, it may be important to define roles for each of the following: caseworker, therapist, foster parent, natural parent, supervisor of caseworker, therapy assistants, court personnel, teachers or school personnel, children, group home coordinator, consultants, medical personnel, and others.

Confidentiality. Because there is close coordination between therapists and agency personnel regarding clients, there must be a clarification of the limits of confidentiality early in the treatment process. What information will be shared by the agency with the therapist and what progress information will be returned to the agency from the therapist are questions that require specific answers. Obviously, given the nature of the problems being addressed, there must be a sharing of information, but there must also be agreement on the extent and type of information to be provided. For example,

- Attendance at therapy sessions
- Compliance with therapy assignments
- Progress through the steps of therapy
- Information shared during therapy (abuse, criminal activity, plans to leave the area)
- Estimation of improvement (likelihood of repeat offenses).

Of course, any agreements reached between the therapist and the agency regarding confidentiality and record keeping must be shared with clients during the initial session.

Support. What level of support will be provided for the therapist by the agency in terms of backup or follow-through for failure to comply with therapy? Many families engage in treatment involuntarily, and it is likely that they may attend sessions but fail to cooperate. This problem will be particularly evident if the referring agency has a history of not following through on threatened consequences. A juvenile court judge who refuses to provide consequences for a juvenile or his or her family members if they agree to treatment but fail to attend beyond the first session removes therapeutic power from the therapist. Or the threat of removing a child from the family and placing him or her in a foster home or group home setting loses its power quickly if parents know the judge does not follow through on removing children. The therapist must be able to identify consequences for failure to participate in treatment.

Therapist: I know you are here against your will — you would prefer to not be here. I can understand that, and under the same circumstances, I'm certain I'd feel the same way. But let me tell you a little about our program. We work with families that have children who manage to get into trouble a good bit. Like your Lucy. It takes us some time and energy working together to help kids get turned around, but we've been pretty successful with about two out of three families. Obviously the juvenile court judge thought Lucy might benefit from the experience and that you are parents who could provide the love and support that she needs to make the changes. Working with us is fairly nonpainful. It requires meeting with us, going over some ideas we'll present, trying them at home, and letting us know how they are working. We'll help fine-tune the methods, and when everything seems to work, then we will stop meeting. We'd like for you to work with us, and give us a chance to help you. On the other hand, if you are so opposed to working with us that you just can't bring yourself to participate in our program, I can understand. If that's your decision, you'll have to let me know so I can advise Child Protective Services that you have chosen to not work with us.

Parent: But if I refuse, they say they'll put Lucy in a group home and we'll have to go to court.

Therapist: Right, I understand that, and that's why we'd really like to work with you, to have you give us the chance to see what we can do. But if you'd rather go the group home route, we'll let you make that decision. But we'd like for you to give us a try instead. Either way, we have to contact Child Protective Services, either to tell them that you will be working with us or that you have declined our services. Would you like to talk further about what we'll do? Maybe if I describe our program in more detail, it will help you decide.

Coordination of Services. Because there is an overlap between therapeutic endeavors and agency responsibilities, it is important that activities be coordinated. We have found, in working with Child Protective Services, that a bimonthly meeting of therapists and caseworkers is crucial for reviewing cases and identifying problems that need to be addressed. This is particularly important considering the population we counsel. We have found, for example, that once therapy is underway, we may know more about the families of aggressive children than their caseworkers do, for we are in contact with the family at least weekly and at times even more often. Families have notified us of weekly moves from one residence to another over several weeks, but because caseworkers may have less frequent contact, at times they do not know the whereabouts of the families. Also, therapists need to be able to communicate to caseworkers needs the family may have that are beyond the mandate of therapy: food stamps, shelter, employment, medical attention. The bimonthly meeting provides this opportunity.

As a therapist, it can be beneficial to develop a liaison relationship with various social service agencies in the community. This liaison or consultant status offers the therapist or clinic representative an opportunity to assist the agencies in case dispositions that will result in an appropriate placement for the client. The therapist can offer insights into what types of treatment appear to be most successful with particular concerns, and whether group, family, individual, or a combination of treatments might be the most effective with a given client. The relationship offers two valuable opportunities for the therapist. First, the therapist can gain knowledge regarding alternative placements for their clientele, including group homes, alternative schools, boy's ranches, and so on. Second, the agency and the therapist benefit from a more in-depth understanding of the limitations, strengths, and training of each other. We have also found that weekly telephone calls to the caseworker of record can develop a strong rapport between therapist and agency personnel.

ENSURING MAINTENANCE

When a family has been able to successfully implement the program within the home and carry out a school program or other out-of-home application, it is time to move toward termination. It is important, however, to keep in mind that the program is seeking to bring about a major alteration in the family system, ways the family has learned to behave and interact through generations of development. Treatment should not end abruptly but through several stages of termination.

Moving Toward Closure

In the initial stage of treatment the therapist took major responsibility for the direction of therapy — identifying problem areas with the family, presenting steps to be followed in preparing for success, self-control, discipline, reinforcement, and school applications. After the family has successfully addressed the problems initially defined in conjunction with the therapist, additional areas should be identified by the parents.

Therapist: Terri, your concerns about Jimmy not minding have lessened in that he does comply when you tell him to do something, fairly quickly it seems. Further, he and Evan are fighting less, and he keeps his room straight. You have also been working on school problems, and he seems to be doing better in that area too. I'm wondering, as we continue to work on the school problems, are there other areas that you think need some attention?

Terri: Well, he doesn't get into trouble like he used to, but there are a couple of areas where I have problems. He's terribly sarcastic. He just seems to have to make a sarcastic or critical statement any time someone says something to him. That gets really aggravating and causes others to dislike him, but he's done it for years and we've just not paid attention to it because there were so many other hassles. The other thing is I'm worried about some of the other kids in the neighborhood — there are some really trashy people living in the area and Jimmy seems to think some of the things they do are cool. I don't know what to do about it.

Therapist: A couple of good areas to address, it sounds like. Let's discuss them in more detail, and then I'd like for you to begin to develop a program to use, what to do, based on what you've done earlier.

At this point the role begins to change from the therapist being the "expert" in charge of telling the family what to do, to having the family become the authority with the therapist becoming more of a coach or consultant. The family develops the intervention program for the next round of treatment, and the therapist advises them or helps them fine-tune their efforts.

The therapist's move from expert to coach serves three major functions:

1. It allows the therapist to observe how well the family is functioning, including providing valuable information about how well they understand the program and the implementation steps.
2. It provides the family with practice within a guided structure so that they may experience success but also have the support and encouragment of the therapist.
3. It allows for a shift in responsibility, with the therapist clearly communicating to the family that they are responsible for their health.

Reducing Contact

Once the family is able to demonstrate an ability to establish the next round of treatment steps and begin implementation, it is possible to move to less frequent contacts, perhaps every 2 weeks instead of weekly.

The therapist may want to alternate meetings in the clinic with phone contacts. The family must not be abruptly cut off from contacts with the therapist, because the changes are not likely to be a stable component of the family style at this stage of treatment. Indeed, the environmental circumstances that initially exacerbated child behavior problems in the family will still be in operation and will influence the family in an adverse manner if therapeutic support is discontinued.

Following Termination

On making the decision that the family is ready to terminate — that is, that they have been able to successfully implement several interventions and have demonstrated competence in child management — the therapist should arrange for follow-up evaluations to determine the extent of change that has occurred. Several forms in the index are useful for that purpose, as well as the standardized instruments described in chapter 4.

Once evaluations have been completed, the therapist should arrange for "booster sessions" to provide continued follow-up of treatment. Our experience has been that families may terminate with successful experiences, but even though attention has been paid to shifting responsibility from the therapist to the family, there is likely to be backsliding within a few weeks. Allowing members of the family to deal with problems on their own for a few months allows them to identify particular areas in which they may need additional support or assistance.

A booster session is scheduled for between the second and third months. We have found that this period of time is sufficient for certain problems to reemerge but that the family has not become too discouraged to be receptive to assistance. The family is contacted and asked to return for a booster session to review what has happened in the last few months. We work with the family members to reinstitute treatment lessons so they can bring about the positive interactions they had had previous to termination. Booster sessions usually run two to three sessions. Once families are again functioning effectively following these sessions, they seem to be able to maintain progress without further contact.

Chapter 11
Program Considerations and Evaluation of Treatment

The treatment program has been used in a variety of settings by diverse therapeutic agents:

- A university research program designed to evaluate treatment effectiveness and implementation (Sayger, Horne, Passmore, & Walker, 1988)
- A university-coordinated home-based family therapy intervention program designed to carry treatment into the home (Boyer & Horne, 1988; Horne, Boyer, Sayger, & Passmore, 1988, October; Horne & Fuelle, 1981)
- Child Protective Services (CPS) caseworkers offering the program through a welfare department service program
- Intensive caseworkers providing a home-based treatment program through a 13-county welfare department program
- Elementary counselors offering the program through the public elementary schools in their area
- Mental health settings (Fleischman & Horne, 1979; Fleischman, Horne, & Arthur, 1983)
- Outpatient child psychiatric facilities (Sayger & Szykula, 1987; Szykula, Sayger, Morris, & Sudweeks, 1987).

IMPROVING SUCCESS

The therapeutic steps presented are intended to be adapted to fit the needs of the therapist using the program, the circumstances of the family, and agency conditions. Although it has been found that a number of intervention programs can be effective with middle-income, two-parent, healthy families that need some corrective assistance with parenting issues (Patterson, 1982), the more intensive the problem areas the family experiences, the more intensive the treatment needs to be.

CONTRAINDICATIONS FOR TREATMENT

The treatment model presented in this book is a comprehensive program for addressing the issues of families with conduct- or oppositional-defiant-disordered children. The clinician should keep in mind, however, that this therapeutic approach is not suited to all clients, and, in fact, we suggest that this model is contraindicated for some families. Kazdin (1987) stated that the conceptualization of treatment is critical and therapists should identify those factors in treatment that address the child's dysfunction. Because treatment should contain specific techniques or procedures for changing behavioral disorders and the etiological factors from which they originate, we suggest that the model of treatment outlined in this book not be the initial intervention with alcoholic or chemically abusive families. In such families, the optimal treatment intervention is directed toward alleviating or controlling alcohol or drug abuse. Therefore, when a conduct- or oppositional-defiant-disordered child or their parent with a chemical dependency is referred for treatment, we seek counseling services for them through alcohol detoxification or drug abuse programs. Once the chemical dependency has been successfully treated, therapy to address child behavioral problems can commence. We have found it useful to contract with such clients for random drug screening tests to be conducted at our request to ensure a drug-free counseling experience.

SPECIAL POPULATIONS

The diagnoses of conduct or oppositional defiant disorders encompass a wide variety of disruptive, antisocial child behaviors. As a result of this wide-ranging categorization, there are specific groups of childhood and adolescent behaviors that require additional attention. These groups include fire setters, stealers, physical abusers, juvenile offenders, and runaways.

Fleischman et al. (1983) note that the therapist must gain a clear identification of these problems through assessing the extent of the concern and specifying exactly what behaviors will be considered part of this classification. These authors (Fleischman et al., 1983) offer the following model for treating fire-setting and stealing behavior.

1. Setting up for success:
    a. Decrease the amount of free time the child has
    b. Enable children to earn items they want by providing jobs or an allowance
    c. Reinforce social interaction for the child who may be socially withdrawn; participation in a structured group or activity would be appropriate.
2. Self-control:
    a. Attempt to end parents "catastrophizing," worrying, and anger
    b. Affirm self-statements such as, they don't approve of the behaviors, they are learning to deal effectively with the behaviors, and the child will change.
3. Discipline:
    a. Assign one or two hours of extra chores per incident
    b. There should be no privileges until the work is done satisfactorily (i.e., no fun, no food, no friends, no phone)
    c. For stealers, face the victim, return what was taken if possible, and apologize
    d. Make whole or partial resititution.
4. Reinforcement:
    a. Develop parallel programs to address other problems so parents have an opportunity to provide positive reinforcement, as reinforcement is inappropriate for expected behaviors such as not stealing, setting fires, or lying
    b. Plan and organize family activities to include all family members; parents should not overdo planning since most adolescents prefer to spend time with peers
    c. Therapists should maintain contact with the parents for at least two months, since parents tend to overlook recurrences of behaviors. (pp. 237–241)

Fire Setters

Fire setting has been identified as one of the more serious aspects of deviant child behavior, and although much has been written explaining the behavior, ranging from psychodynamic, social-environmental, and family interactions explanations, much less has been written about treatment approaches, particularly in a noninstitutionalized setting. Much recent work has been done, however, directing practitioners in ways of identifying and classifying firesetters (Kolko & Kazdin, 1988; Kolko, Kazdin, & Meyer, 1985; Last, Griest, & Kazdin, 1985; Sakheim, Vigdor, Gordon, & Helprin, 1985). In general, fire setters seem to engage in more delinquent and antisocial behaviors than non-fire setters, and they evidence greater social skills deficits and a broad range of aggressive behaviors beyond their primary symptoms (Kolko & Kazdin, 1986; Kolko et al., 1985). Although all forms of conduct disorder warrant attention and treatment, fire-setting behavior calls for early identification, diagnosis, and treatment, for the more extended the period of practice, the more difficult it is to treat and the more the severity of the problem increases.

Schaefer, Briesmeister, and Fitton (1986) state that a family systems approach to treatment would view the development of fire-setting behavior within the context of the family and note that it may serve one or more purposes within the family (e.g., fire setting may be initiated and maintained to keep the focus off marital problems or to keep the parents together). If this is the case, the treatment model presented in this book should be appropriately refocused to stress more directly the conflictual marital relationship.

To clearly specify what constitutes fire-setting behavior the parents should note the following occurrences:

1. Setting fires — no matter how small
2. Playing with matches
3. Having possession of matches or a lighter
4. Being in the presence of someone else who lights a fire or plays with matches
5. Failure to account for their presence or having their location verified by a trustworthy person during a time when a fire was set.

Stealers

Wells and Forehand (1985) note that parent-training treatment for children who engage in "predelinquent" behaviors, such as stealing, becomes complicated by the fact that the presenting problem at the time of referral is usually aversive and aggressive behaviors in the home. The stealing behavior has many times not been observed by the parent because the child has become effective at concealing such transgressions. Patterson (1982) stated that parents of stealers display two distinct characteristics in their parenting practices. First, they tend to be relatively uninvolved in the role of caretaker and distant or unattached in their relationships with their children. Second, these parents tend to lack concern for property violations, for example, ignoring minor violations that occur in the home (viz., taking money from the mother's purse, borrowing items from siblings without asking permission). In a study on children referred to the Oregon Social Learning Center, Patterson (1982) found that 72% of the children who disobeyed were also likely to lie, 32% who stole were also said by their parents to set fires, and 70% who stole also lied. According to Patterson's frequency labeling hypothesis, children who are between the ages of 6 and 12 years and are caught stealing once every 3 or 4 months are labeled stealers. The prognosis for children identified as high-rate stealers, who are also lacking in social skills, is not positive. These children are at a greater risk for becoming career offenders and being prosecuted for their offenses.

Fleischman et al. (1983) state that the following behaviors should be identified as stealing when establishing a treatment program for stealers:

1. Taking anything that is not theirs, regardless of its value
2. Possessing any item for which they cannot prove ownership, including items the child states he or she "found" or "borrowed"
3. Being present when someone else steals anything
4. Being accused of stealing something and failing to have their presence elsewhere verified by a trustworthy person.

Abusive Families

From the perspective of our treatment program, child physical abuse is seen as an outgrowth of particular parental deficiencies, stress, and isolation. Parental deficiencies may include inadequate skill at managing stress, ignorance of normal child development with resulting unrealistic expectations for the child, inability to teach or encourage appropriate behavior, and a lack of effective alternatives to physical punishment for the child.

It is also not uncommon for abusive families to be subjected to stress from a variety of sources. Parents may frequently experience depression, anxiety, and uncontrollable anger. There may also be stressors within or outside the family (e.g., marital conflicts, alcohol or drug abuse, extended-family problems, nonsupportive friendships). And, as is common concern for many abusive families, environmental stressors such as poverty, unemployment, single parenting, or inadequate housing can create an atmosphere that is conducive to abusive behaviors.

Typically, abusive families experience a great deal of isolation from friends, family, and community resources, which exacerbates the parents' inability to find time away from the child. For many parents, the child becomes a substitute for other social contacts with adults, and the parent is deprived of the opportunity to observe more effective parenting styles or share concerns and information about parenting. And, as many of us are aware, isolation provides an atmosphere in which the abusive family can hide parenting behaviors that would otherwise not be condoned by society.

Wolfe and Sandler (1981) examined child-abusing families and discovered certain patterns of family interaction. The primary determinant for child abuse may be an abusive parent who uses excessive and inappropriate discipline, an abuse-prone child who contributes to the probability of abuse by exhibiting aggressive, antisocial behaviors, and/or an abusive partnership consisting of mutually hostile and competitive behavior between parent and child.

Otto and Smith (1980) proposed a six-phase cognitive behavioral intervention for working with child-abusing families. The six phases include:

1. A crisis intervention stage focused on stopping the current abusive sequence with a corresponding deescalation of feelings
2. A cognitive restructuring step which seeks to eliminate the myth that most parents enjoy parenting and find it easy, natural, and rewarding
3. Reeducating parents concerning normal developmental expectations for their child and thus uncovering unrealistic expectations
4. Linking children and parents with appropriate therapeutic programs; these may include individual, group, marital, and/or family therapy
5. Developing alternative and more constructive family norms and identities which can serve to increase self-esteem
6. Refocusing therapy from cognitive behavior therapy to more traditional psychotherapy if necessary.

It is our experience that a multiple modality treatment approach is most effective for working with abusive families. For example, parents may attend a parent-training group, couples therapy, and family therapy with their child. The child would be involved in a support group for abused children as well as individual therapy and family therapy. The abusing parent would also be involved in individual therapy to address issues of anger and inappropriate interactions with the child.

Fleischman et al. (1983) note that, when treating abusive families, the early focus of treatment should be on self-control and child management skills. Later stages of treatment could focus on environmental stressors as needed. In providing treatment, the therapist maintains an obligation to report any suspected abuse and should be in consistent contact with the family's caseworker. It has been our experience that it is best not to have the caseworker involved directly in providing treatment, because social service agencies have the potential to recommend legal sanctions that would negatively affect the trust between the client and caseworker.

Juvenile Offenders

Juvenile offenders are difficult individuals with whom to work as therapists confront such issues as extremely short-term treatment programs, (initial offenders are detained in detention facilities for only short periods of time), inability to include most families in treatment, severe client deficits in multiple skill areas, and inconsistency in court dispositions. Most juveniles commit crimes for excitement or immediate gratification with little consideration for the possible consequences. Community-based treatment for juvenile offenders is generally cheaper than residential care and creates less disruption in the child's family life, schooling, peer group interactions, and other developmental experiences (Jones, 1987). Many juvenile court judges utilize diversion strategies as a cost-effective deterrent to continued criminality. These strategies may include community service, restitution, attending therapy, or a simple reprimand.

Peryea (1989) suggested that the primary gap in counseling services for conduct disorders appears to be at the level of adolescence. There is a general consensus among professionals working with juvenile offenders that once conduct-disordered children are seen in multiple settings and over time, intervention is increasingly unsuccessful. Peryea (1989) also stated that a social learning family therapy model could be a very effective approach in treating the concerns of juvenile offenders if the family is available and willing to participate in therapy. To date, most treatment programs have focused on providing social skills training for the offending juvenile; however, a comprehensive and flexible family therapy model combined with social skills training might provide the most effective treatment intervention for juveniles in community-based programs, residential facilities, or diversion strategies.

Runaways

Adams and Adams (1987) noted that few professionals are trained to deal with the often difficult and frustrating group of runaway children and their families. These authors proposed that the identification of a runaway youth should include the following information: (a) age of the youth, (b) absence of parental or guardian permission, (c) a criterion for length of absence from the home. It appears that children who experience weak bonding with the family or other social groups along with exposure to deviant social behavior are at a greater risk for running away. Runaways are typically characterized by insecurity, low self-esteem, unhappiness or depression, impulsiveness, and a chaotic personal life. Adams and Adams (1987) provided the following assumptions regarding runaways:

1. Runaway youth are not a homogeneous group
2. Runaway behavior is a problem in its own right and is also symptomatic of other problems

3. Runaway behavior represents a continuum of responses ranging from a pattern of chronic maladaption to a fundamentally healthy reaction to a pathological environment
4. Runaway behavior may have multiple causal and contributory factors
5. There are identifiable subgroups of runaway youth representing distinct populations of runaways, each requiring markedly different intervention efforts
6. Effective intervention with runaways requires accurate assessment of the problems that appear etiologically linked to the runaway behavior.

Treatment for these youths should include an initial crisis intervention and an attempt to obtain a stabilized placement, supportive counseling, and appropriate education and training. Occasionally, long-term therapy may be required.

The previous sections offer brief descriptions of various behavioral concerns that clinicians may need to address. The treatment approach outlined in this book may need to be altered, expanded, or used in combination with other approaches to satisfactorily assess and treat these special populations.

EVALUATION OF TREATMENT

The evaluation, development, and refinement of the family treatment model presented in this book has been in progress for several years. The model has been utilized in a variety of clinical settings and with varying severity of diagnoses. This section will present some of the research conducted on the efficacy of this family therapy model for alleviating diagnostic concerns for families with conduct- or oppositional-defiant-disordered children.

Family Therapy Applications

Sayger (1987), Walker (1985), and Sayger, Horne, and Walker (1987) have examined the effectiveness of a social learning family therapy model for treating conduct and oppositional defiant disorders in children. Each of these studies determined that the treatment program, with treatment fidelity rigidly assessed, was effective in reducing a variety of deviant child behaviors in both the home and the school.

Walker (1985) and Sayger et al. (1987) noted that following the course of treatment outlined in this book was effective in reducing the highly aggressive behaviors of conduct- and oppositional-defiant-disordered children between the ages of 6 and 12 years. Children were referred for participation in these studies by elementary school personnel. Analyses of data from these treatment outcome investigations revealed a significant reduction in aggressive, acting-out behaviors of the child. Walker (1985) stated that the boys participating in his study evidenced a 48% reduction in aggressive, disruptive behaviors in the classroom.

In a reexamination and follow-up of families participating in the Walker (1985) study, Sayger et al. (1988) discovered that positive treatment effects were also shown to have occurred in many family systems variables, including family cohesion, total family relationship, reduction of family conflict, and mood and tone. In addition, family problem-solving abilities improved during and following treatment as families demonstrated a capacity to utilize positive solution behaviors when discussing family concerns (see Table 11.1 on pages 140–141).

In an examination of prosocial behaviors, Sayger et al. (1988) determined that such child behaviors as doing homework without arguing, complying, happiness, and playing appropriately also increased during and following treatment. Deviant school behavior was also shown to decrease during the course of treatment with maintenance at follow-up (see Table 11.2 on page 142).

Van Valkenburg (1986), in a review of predictors of treatment outcome for the Walker (1985) study, noted that a collective set of demographic, parent, and therapist variables were not predictive of treatment outcome. However, all families in the treatment program reported positive treatment gains, and thus the analyses were not able to distinguish between those families and children that demonstrated high gains versus those that improved but demonstrated lower gains.

Szykula, Sayger, Morris, and Sudweeks (1987) noted that 100% of the families of children referred to an outpatient psychiatric setting and participating in a social learning family therapy approach demonstrated gains toward their treatment attainment goals. Sayger, Szykula, Sudweeks, Morris, and Child (1987, November) asked parents to report on the possible side effects of treatment and discovered that they cited significantly more positive side effects from participation in social learning family therapy than negative ones. Parents reported positive changes in their marital relationship, interactions between siblings, and their self-esteem, even though these areas were not the primary focus of treatment.

Sayger, Horne, and Glaser (1989) investigated the impact of a social learning family therapy program for child conduct disorders on the level of marital satisfaction between parents. Using the Locke–Wallace Marital Adjustment Test (LWMAT) (Locke & Wallace, 1959), these researchers noted that couples who reported low marital satisfaction before treatment achieved a normal level of marital satisfaction after treatment.

Table 11.1. Results of the One-Way Analyses of Variance with Repeated Measures for Pre-, Post-, and Follow-up Assessments on Family Environment or Relationship and Problem-Solving Variables

Instrument, Subscale, and Source	DF	Sum of Squares	Mean Squares	F Ratio	Probability
Family Environment Scale					
Total relationship					
Between groups	2	11,040.03	5,520.02	7.36	.001
Within groups	57	42,755.70	750.10		
Total	59	53,795.73			
Cohesion					
Between groups	2	1,987.60	993.80	4.30	.018
Within groups	57	13,175.80	231.15		
Total	59	15,163.40			
Expressiveness					
Between groups	2	539.20	269.60	1.77	.180
Within Groups	57	8,690.05	152.46		
Total	59	9,229.25			
Conflict					
Between groups	2	1,490.23	745.17	4.60	.014
Within groups	57	9,240.35	162.11		
Total	59	10,730.58			
Beavers–Timberlawn Family Evaluation Scale					
Expressiveness					
Between groups	2	7.43	3.71	7.61	.001
Within groups	57	27.80	0.49		
Total	59	35.23			
Mood and Tone					
Between groups	2	5.64	2.82	7.50	.001
Within groups	57	21.43	0.38		
Total	59	27.07			
Conflict					
Between groups	2	8.57	4.28	6.64	.003
Within groups	57	36.76	0.64		
Total	59	45.33			
Empathy					
Between groups	2	2.79	1.40	3.54	.036
Within groups	57	22.53	0.40		
Total	59	25.32			
Global Health/Pathology					
Between groups	2	33.26	16.63	9.97	.001
Within groups	57	95.05	1.67		
Total	59	128.31			
Goal-directed negotiation					
Between groups	2	5.08	2.54	3.83	.027
Within groups	57	37.79	0.66		
Total	59	42.87			
Family Problem-Solving Behavior Coding System					
Positive solution behavior					
Between groups	2	2,567.23	1,283.62	9.07	.001
Within groups	57	8,070.95	141.60		
Total	59	10,638.18			

Table 11.1. *Continued*

Instrument, Subscale, and Source	DF	Sum of Squares	Mean Squares	F Ratio	Probability
Negative solution behavior					
Between groups	2	1,710.63	855.32	7.65	.001
Within groups	57	6,376.10	111.86		
Total	59	8,086.73			
Off-task behavior					
Between groups	2	365.60	187.80	3.03	.056
Within groups	57	3,529.00	61.91		
Total	59	3,904.60			
Problem-solving efficiency					
Between groups	2	12.13	6.07	23.29	.001
Within groups	57	14.85	0.26		
Total	59	26.98			

Couples reporting normal or high levels of marital satisfaction before treatment demonstrated maintenance of these levels.

Group Applications

While the primary application of treatment for families with oppositional-defiant- or conduct-disordered children has been working with one family at a time, group applications have also been used. When using the treatment in a group format, families are met individually for the initial session. During the first contact the treatment model is explained, and intake and evaluation data are collected. Some conditions would restrict assignment to a group format (e.g., severe child abuse, child sexual abuse, or an antisocial child whose behavior is so extreme that the therapist must have regular contact for evaluation purposes).

After the initial session is held with a family, an explanation of the treatment has been presented, and evaluation data have been collected, a second session is held with the entire family present. During this session the Goal Setting Forms are completed, and a treatment program is agreed on by the therapist, parents, and children involved.

Beginning with the third session parents meet in a group with other parents, usually three to five couples to a group. This method works best if the parents participating share common problems with their children so that the group can be used as a resource for treatment ideas. A second consideration for group membership is the likely compatibility of group members (i.e., age, sex, and socioeconomic factors). For example, a teen-age single-parent welfare mother may not benefit as much if she is placed in a group of upper-income, middle-aged couples.

In using a group treatment format it is helpful to have a cotherapist,

Table 11.2. Results of the One-Way Analyses of Variance with Repeated Measures for Pre-, Post-, and Follow-up Scores on Child Behavior Variables

Instrument, Subscale, and Source	DF	Sum of Squares	Mean Squares	F Ratio	Probability
Parent Daily Report					
Positive behavior					
Between groups	2	1,251.10	625.55	3.70	.031
Within groups	57	9,639.75	169.12		
Total	59	10,890.85			
Negative behavior					
Between groups	2	446.40	223.20	4.00	.024
Within groups	57	3,180.20	55.79		
Total	59	3,626.60			
Child Behavior Checklist					
Aggressive					
Between groups	2	1,636.13	818.07	7.35	.001
Within groups	57	6,346.05	111.33		
Total	59	7,982.18			
Hyperactive					
Between groups	2	1,272.90	636.45	6.69	.002
Within groups	57	5,426.70	95.21		
Total	59	6,699.60			
Depressed					
Between groups	2	1,338.23	669.12	6.76	.002
Within groups	57	5,642.35	98.99		
Total	59	6,980.58			
Delinquent					
Between groups	2	586.43	293.22	6.63	.003
Within groups	57	2,521.75	44.24		
Total	59	3,108.18			
Internalizing					
Between groups	2	1,636.63	818.32	5.74	.005
Within group	57	8,125.55	142.55		
Total	59	9,762.18			
Externalizing					
Between groups	2	1,650.23	825.12	7.48	.001
Within groups	57	6,290.75	110.36		
Total	59	7,940.98			
Sum T					
Between groups	2	1,736.23	868.12	7.42	.001
Within groups	57	6,670.35	117.02		
Total	59	8,406.58			
Daily Behavior Checklist					
Total Score					
Between groups	2	2,222.50	1,111.25	13.87	.001
Within groups	57	4,566.50	80.11		
Total	59	6,789.00			

because parents with conduct-disordered children frequently have difficulty in maintaining self-control and the group setting can become quite chaotic. Having a coleader allows one therapist to take the lead role while the other therapist observes group interactions, reactions, and nonverbal responses to treatment.

Group therapy is not only numerically different than individual therapy, it is also conceptually different and requires quite different skills on the part of the therapist. Therapists who are not trained in working with groups should obtain such training before establishing a therapy group for parents who have oppositional-defiant- or conduct-disordered children. A primary difference is that the principal resource for individual treatment is the therapist, whereas in group therapy the major resource is the group itself. For further information on working with a group therapy approach, see Ohlsen, Horne, and Lawe (1988) and Yalom (1985) and, for the specific application of a social learning treatment model to a group format, see Fleischman et al. (1983, chapter 13) and Reid (1989).

Reid (1989) compared treatment outcome for families seen in an individual family format versus families seen in a group family format. He compared 20 families in each type of treatment, examining changes in the Daily Behavior Checklist, Parent Daily Report (PDR), Child Behavior Checklist (CBCL), Family Environment Scale, Beavers–Timberlawn Family Evaluation Scale, Family Problem-Solving Behavior Coding System, Problem-Solving Efficiency Scale, and the LWMAT. Following the initial intake interview, families in the group treatment format met for weekly sessions in groups of three to five families.

Reid (1989) reported that treatment in a group therapy format resulted in significant reduction in home deviant behaviors (PDR and CBCL) and that parents developed improved perceptions of their own children, but that it may not be as effective for addressing such issues as marital conflict and family environment. Reid indicates that parent group applications are time-efficient and cost-effective, for by the end of the treatment condition significant reductions in negative child and family behaviors were found, with corresponding increases in positive behaviors. This was accomplished "with approximately 40 percent fewer client/therapist contact hours" (pp. 161–162).

The group model, however, did not appear to be as effective in generalizing positive change from the family to school behaviors. This was apparently due to the treatment program focusing only on family problems and excluding school issues which required contacting teachers or other school personnel. Treatment evaluations that included teacher ratings of behavior indicated that school problems did not improve. Therapists using a group treatment model should be aware that they will have to either systematically include school issues in the group format or treat these issues separately through individual work with the family.

Another area that failed to show a positive change in a group format as compared to the individual approach was family systems variables. Whereas working with individual families can lead to systemic change (Sayger et al., 1988), these changes were not found using a group approach (Reid, 1989).

It appears that application of this treatment approach in addressing the concerns of conduct- or oppositional-defiant-disordered children reduces negative and increases positive child behaviors and can also have a significant impact on related family and marital variables. These are encouraging findings as one considers the generally chaotic nature of family life when behaviorally deviant children are present.

Appendix A

INTAKE FORM

Date: _____

ID # _____

CHILD

1. **Identified Child's Full Name** _____

2. **Referred by:**   self _____   friend _____   school _____   court _____   agency _____   other _____

3. **Reason for referral:** _____

_____

_____

4. **Other concerns:** _____

_____

5. **Prescription drugs child is taking:** _____   Reasons: _____

6. **Handicaps, Disabilities of Child:** _____

7. **Is the child having problems at school?**   Yes _____   No _____

   If so, please specify: _____

   _____

   How long have these problems existed? _____

   Child's School _____

   Teacher _____   Grade _____

8. **Do you want assistance in resolving school problems?**   Yes _____   No _____

9. **Have you been having problems with the child at home?**   Yes _____   No _____

   If yes, please specify: _____

   _____

   How long have these problems existed? _____

10. **Do you want assistance in resolving home problems?**   Yes _____   No _____

The following behaviors are sometimes seen in children who have problems at home or at school. Please check those that apply to your child.

Does your child often:	No	Yes	Times per week
lose his/her temper?	——	——	——
argue with adults?	——	——	——
defy or refuse adult requests or rules? e.g. refuse to do chores at home	——	——	——
deliberately do things that annoy other people?	——	——	——
blame others for his or her own mistake?	——	——	——
get touchy or easily annoyed by others?	——	——	——
seem angry and resentful?	——	——	——
act spiteful or vindictive?	——	——	——
swear or use obscene language?	——	——	——
lie?	——	——	——
skip school?	——	——	——
initiate physical fights?	——	——	——

Has your child: *Please check those that apply to your child*	No	Yes	No. of times
run away from home overnight?	——	——	——
stolen without confronting another person? e.g. shoplifting, school materials	——	——	——
stolen while confronting another person? e.g. mugging, purse-snatching	——	——	——
broken into someone's house, building or car?	——	——	——
deliberately destroyed others' property? (not fires)	——	——	——
deliberately set fires?	——	——	——
been physically cruel to animals?	——	——	——
been physically cruel to people?	——	——	——
used a weapon in more than one fight?	——	——	——

FAMILY

1. **Parents/Guardians Names:**

   Mr. _____   Age _____

   Mrs. _____   Age _____

   Address/Mom: _____   Address/Dad: _____
                   Street or P.O. Box   Street or P.O. Box

   _____   _____
   City   State   Zip Code   City   State   Zip Code

   Phone Mom: _____   Phone Dad: _____

   If no phone, at what number can the family be contacted? _____

2. **Marital Status:** _____ single   _____ married   _____ separated

                        _____ divorced   _____ widowed   _____ other

   Date of Marriage   Years Married   Reason for Termination of Marriage

   _____   _____   _____ death _____ divorce _____ other

   _____   _____   _____ death _____ divorce _____ other

   _____   _____   _____ death _____ divorce _____ other

3. **Race/Ethnic Origin:** Mother _____   Father _____

4. **Education:** *(Circle highest grade level completed)*

   Mother: Grade: 6 7 8 9 10 11 12   Technical School: 1 2   College: 1 2 3 4 Advanced

   Father: Grade: 6 7 8 9 10 11 12   Technical School: 1 2   College: 1 2 3 4 Advanced

5. **Occupation:** Job Description   Currently Employed?   Where?

   Mother: _____   _____ Yes _____ No   _____

   Father: _____   _____ Yes _____ No   _____

   Approximate Annual Family Income: _____

6. **Other significant family members residing in the home** (residential grandparents, other relatives) or having a relationship to the child (biological father/mother living outside the home).

   Name _____   Relationship _____

   Name _____   Relationship _____

   Name _____   Relationship _____

7. **Number of Children living at home:** _____

Name: _____   Age: _____   Sex: (M,F) ____

_____   _____   ____

_____   _____   ____

_____   _____   ____

_____   _____   ____

8. **Are any of the other children having problems?**   Yes _____   No _____
If yes, please specify:

_____

_____

_____

9. **Previous counseling received by family members:**

For which family member   Reason for counseling

____ Individual, please describe: _____   _____

____ Marital, please describe: _____   _____

____ Family, please describe: _____   _____

10. **Other information:** (positive qualities of the child/parents, relationships with other children, relationships with agencies, neighbors, relatives, etc.)

11. **Attach a copy of the case plan.**

Family Intake Form
Part A

FAMILY
Name: _____
ID: _____
Address: _____
Phone: _____

Household Members	Sex	DOB Age	Marital Status	Ethnic Group	Relationship to Client 1	Risk of Placement	Living Arrang.	Employment Status	Employer	Educ. Status	School	Teacher	Referral Service	Child Placement History	Dates of Previous Services
1. (Parent)															
2.															
3.															
4.															
5.															
6.															
7.															
8.															
9.															
10.															

150

Part B: Codes

Sex
F – Female
M – Male

Marital Status (MS)
D – Divorced
M – Married
L – Separated, legal
P – Separated, other
S – Single
W – Widowed
U – Unknown

Ethnic Group (EG)
B – Black
N – Native-American
H – Hispanic
A – Asian
W – White

Relationship to Client #1
S – Present spouse
X – Former spouse
P – Parent
A – Adoptive parent, nonrelated
W – Stepparent
J – Alleged father, not adjudicated
F – Foster parent
H – Foster sibling
L – Sibling
R – Other relative
C – Child
T – Adoptive child
B – Stepchild
D – Foster child
O – Other, nonrelative
X – Other, relative

Living Arrangement (LA)
AH – Adoptive home
LI – Living independently
LR – Adult living in house of relative
CP – Child living with parents
CR – Child living with other relative
PI – Correctional facility
FG – Foster home
FP – Foster home, permanent
GF – Group home, family
GA – Group residence, agency
RF – Residential care
OO – Other:

Educational Status (ES)
0 – Preschool
1 – Attending school, if not attending, highest level completed
2 – Less than 8th grade
3 – Junior high
4 – High school
5 – Vocational
6 – Junior college
7 – College
8 – Graduate/professional

Risk for Placement (RP)
1 – No risk
2 – Minimal risk
3 – Moderate risk
4 – High risk

Employment Status
FP – Full permanent
FT – Full temporary
FS – Full seasonal
PT – Part permanent
PS – Part seasonal
US – Seeking
U – Student
UH – Home
UR – Retired
UD – Disabled
UL – Laid off
UT – Other
XX – Unknown

Referral Source
B – Clergy
O – Probation Officer
P – Medical
A – Social agency
C – Court
L – Law enforcement agency
U – Other organization
R – Relative
E – School
J – Client interest group
X – Unknown

Factors Contributing to Change Scale

Case ID #: _____   Interview: _____   Date: _____

Instructions: Select the rating that is the most accurate for each parent. If you do not have adequate information or if the item is not applicable, put N/A. It will be helpful to review this information when the parents are present in order to clarify any items for which you may lack information.

					Scores	
					Mother	Father
Access to transportation:	1 Lacking	2	3 Some difficulty	4	5 Reliable	_____ _____
Access to phone:	1 Extremely limited	2	3 Inconvenient	4	5 Readily accessible	_____ _____
Daily schedule:	1 Changes drastically	2	3 Predictable	4	5 Very routine	_____ _____
Family stability:	1 Chaotic	2	3 Some stability	4	5 Stable	_____ _____
Social support for parent:	1 Discourages participation	2	3 Uninvolved	4	5 Encourages parents	_____ _____
Parent social relations:	1 Few or negative	2	3 All right	4	5 Positive	_____ _____
Child social relations:	1 Few or negative	2	3 All right	4	5 Positive	_____ _____

152

	1	2	3	4	5		
Cooperation of other agencies:	No support	2	Neutral	4	Supportive	—	—
Parent's mental health:	Severe disturbance	2	Minor disturbance	4	No problems	—	—
Parent's extended family:	Nonsupportive	2	Neutral	4	Supportive	—	—
Use of discipline/ parent's family: Bruises/welts?	Corporal discipline Y N	2	3	4	No spanking/ yelling	—	—
Current use of discipline:	Corporal discipline	2	3	4	No spanking/ yelling	—	—
Parent's philosophy or religious views:	Incompatible with model	2	Somewhat compatible with model	4	Compatible with model	—	—
Insularity of mother:	Child is only person with parent	2	One adult companion	4	Many adult companions	—	—
Parental time available with child/day:	Almost none	2	Some	4	Several hours daily	—	—
Parental time spent with friends/week:	None	2	Some	4	Several times a week	—	—

153

Factors Contributing to Change Scale (Continued)

	1	2	3	4	5	Scores Mother	Father
Perception of neighborhood:	Terrible	2	All right	4	Wonderful	_____	_____
Crises currently facing family:	One or more	2	None currently	4	None foreseen	_____	_____
Competing demands:	Several	2	Some	4	None	_____	_____
Possibility of child's removal from home:	Very likely	2	Possible	4	Unlikely	_____	_____
Parent perception of research project:	Negative	2	Neutral	4	Positive	_____	_____

Interviewer Assessment: To be completed after the family assessment session

	1	2	3	4	5	Scores Mother	Father
Parent's mental ability:	Extremely slow	2	Average	4	Very intelligent	_____	_____
Problem awareness: Parent	See no problems	2	Suspect problems	4	Aware of problems	_____	_____
Child	See no problems	2	Suspect problems	4	Aware of problems	_____	_____

154

Comfort with self-disclosure:

	1	2	3	4	5
Parent	Very concerned		Some concern		Highly trusting
Child	Very concerned		Some concern		Highly trusting
Parent's willingness to expend effort:	Clear reluctance		Some reluctance		Highly willing
Parent's sensitivity to seeking help:	Very concerned		Hesitant		No problems
Parent's attribution of problem:	Illness		Unsure		Interaction with child
Parent's desire for enhanced parenting skills:	None		Some		Desire improvement
Interviewer's opinion of family:	Disliked		Neutral		Liked

Likelihood of progress:

	1	2	3	4	5
Parent	Highly unlikely		Unlikely		Very likely
Therapist	Highly unlikely		Unlikely		Very likely
Rapid benefits:	Highly unlikely		Unlikely		Very likely

Post-Factors Contributing to Change Scale

Case ID #: _____

Therapist: _____

Date: _____

Instructions: Select the rating that is the most accurate for each parent. If you do not have adequate information or if item is not applicable, put N/A.

	Hindered		Neither contributed nor detracted		Facilitated	Scores Mother	Father
Access to transportation:	1	2	3	4	5	_____	_____
Access to phone:	1	2	3	4	5	_____	_____
Daily schedule:	1	2	3	4	5	_____	_____
Family stability:	1	2	3	4	5	_____	_____
Social support for parent:	1	2	3	4	5	_____	_____
Parental social relations:	1	2	3	4	5	_____	_____
Child social relations:	1	2	3	4	5	_____	_____
Family's reasons for entry into treatment:	1	2	3	4	5	_____	_____
Child's reasons for entry into treatment:	1	2	3	4	5	_____	_____
Program expectations:	1	2	3	4	5	_____	_____
Cooperation of other agencies:	1	2	3	4	5	_____	_____
Parents' mental health:	1	2	3	4	5	_____	_____
Parent's ability to work together:	1	2	3	4	5	_____	_____
Parent's belief about reinforcement:	1	2	3	4	5	_____	_____
Parent's belief about behavioral treatment:	1	2	3	4	5	_____	_____
Parents' previous use of discipline:	1	2	3	4	5	_____	_____
Parents' philosophy or religious views:	1	2	3	4	5	_____	_____

Post-Factors Contributing to Change Scale (Continued)

	Hindered	Neither contributed nor detracted			Facilitated	Scores Mother	Father
Parent's understanding of treatment requirements:	1	2	3	4	5	_____	_____
Parent's mental ability:	1	2	3	4	5	_____	_____
Parent's willingness to expend effort:	1	2	3	4	5	_____	_____
Parent's sensitivity to seeking help:	1	2	3	4	5	_____	_____
Parents' attribution of problems:	1	2	3	4	5	_____	_____
Parents' desire for enhanced parenting skills:	1	2	3	4	5	_____	_____
Insularity of mother:	1	2	3	4	5	_____	_____
Possibility of child's removal from home:	1	2	3	4	5	_____	_____
At intake, child's reaction to treatment:	1	2	3	4	5	_____	_____
Parental time available with child/day:	1	2	3	4	5	_____	_____
Crises currently facing family:	1	2	3	4	5	_____	_____
Competing demands:	1	2	3	4	5	_____	_____
Problem awareness: Parent:	1	2	3	4	5	_____	_____
Child:	1	2	3	4	5	_____	_____
Comfort with self-disclosure: Parent	1	2	3	4	5	_____	_____
Child	1	2	3	4	5	_____	_____
Parental perception of therapist competence:	1	2	3	4	5	_____	_____
Parental perception of research project:	1	2	3	4	5	_____	_____
Therapist's opinion of family:	1	2	3	4	5	_____	_____
Therapist's opinion of child:	1	2	3	4	5	_____	_____

Appendix A

Post-Factors Contributing to Change Scale (Continued)

	Hindered	Neither contributed nor detracted			Facilitated	Scores Mother	Father
Likelihood of progress: Therapist	1	2	3	4	5	_____	_____
Family	1	2	3	4	5	_____	_____
Pace of treatment:	1	2	3	4	5	_____	_____
Therapist's opinion of treatment outcome:	1	2	3	4	5	_____	_____
Setting up for success:	1	2	3	4	5	_____	_____
Self-control:	1	2	3	4	5	_____	_____
Contingent reinforcement techniques:	1	2	3	4	5	_____	_____
Contingent discipline techniques:	1	2	3	4	5	_____	_____
Communication:	1	2	3	4	5	_____	_____
School intervention:	1	2	3	4	5	_____	_____

Therapist Termination Report

Date _____

Therapist name: _____

Family

    Name _____

    Case # _____

    Address _____

    Phone # _____

    Child's name _____

    Case ID# _____

Treatment started _____

Treatment completed _____

Number of visits scheduled _____

Number of visits occurring _____

No shows/refusals _____

Clinical hours:
Direct time working with this family _____

Indirect time working with this family _____

Time spent on school issues _____

Number of family contacts with parents and child _____

Number of family contacts with parents only _____

Number of family contacts with child only _____

Number of school-related contacts _____

1. What was the family's status at termination? (Check one.)

    Although therapist would have preferred their remaining in treatment, _____
family quit treatment during <u>initial</u> phase (first three sessions).

    Although therapist would have preferred their remaining in treatment, _____
family quit treatment during <u>middle</u> phase (more than three sessions, less than eight).

    Although therapist would have preferred their remaining in treatment, _____
family quit treatment during <u>latter</u> phase (eight or more sessions).

    Case permanently interrupted because of <u>circumstances beyond control</u> _____
of family or therapist. Explain.

    The decision to terminate was <u>mutually agreed</u> on even though many or _____
all of the referral problems <u>still existed</u>.

    The decision to terminate was <u>mutually agreed</u> on because many or all _____
of the referral problems were <u>resolved</u>. Other problems, however, still remained. Cite.

    Case was terminated with referral problems <u>well resolved</u>. No major _____
problems remained.

Therapist Termination Report (Continued)

2. In which areas was your assistance directly focused? (Check as many as appropriate).

Alcohol/drug problems	_____
Child management/parent training	_____
Family communication	_____
Marital problems	_____
Assertiveness/social isolation	_____
Depression	_____
Fear or anxieties	_____
School problems	_____
Other (specify): _____	

3. Which of the following was included in your treatment? (Check as many as appropriate, but rank them: 1, 2, 3, etc., according to amount of time on each.)

Setting up for success	_____
Effective discipline:	
Time-out	_____
Grandma's law	_____
Natural/logical consequences	_____
Assigning chores	_____
Withholding attention	_____
Taking away privileges	_____
Communication	_____
Generalization	_____
Self-control (parents)	_____
Self-control (child)	_____
Effective reinforcement:	
Social	_____
Point system	_____
Contracts	_____
Allowances	_____
School issues	_____
Maintenance	_____

4. Did you use any other social learning or behavior-oriented procedures but not as presented in the troubled family therapy book? If yes, which:

5. Did treatment involve assistance with some additional form of service?
Yes _____ No _____
If yes, in which of the following areas did you assist the family?
(Check as many as appropriate.)

Alcohol/drug abuse	_____	Custody issues	_____
Day care services	_____	Employment	_____
Homemaker services	_____	Housing assistance	_____
Job training	_____	Legal assistance	_____
Welfare (Specify what)	_____	Termination of parental rights	_____
Shelter care, foster care,		Medical/dental services	_____
group home placement	_____		
Other (be specific): _____			

Therapist Termination Report (Continued)

6. At any point during treatment, was this child or family receiving other forms of therapy or counseling? If yes, which? (Check as many as appropriate.)

Family doctor (for child behavioral or
    parent emotional problems) _____
Other therapist (psychologist,
    counselor) _____
Special school services _____
Other (specify): _____

Clergy _____
Psychiatrist _____
Children's services division _____
Juvenile court _____

7. At termination was the family receiving any additional assistance? Yes ___ No ___
If yes, which? (Check as many as appropriate.)

Family doctor (for child behavioral or
    parent emotional problems) _____
Other therapist (psychologist,
    counselor) _____
Special school services _____
Other (specify): _____

Clergy _____
Psychiatrist _____
Children's services division _____
Juvenile court _____

8. To your knowledge was the target child ever physically abused or neglected?

Before treatment? (Check one.)
    Abused _____
    Neglected _____
    Neither _____

During treatment? (Check one.)
    Abused _____
    Neglected _____
    Neither _____

How certain are you of your ratings on this item? (Check one.)

Not sure at all _____ Moderately sure _____ Certain _____

9. Was the target child placed out of the home?

No _____

Yes _____
Before treatment _____
During treatmet _____
Following treatment _____

10. Were other children placed out of the home?

No _____

Yes _____
Before treatment _____
During treatment _____
Following treatment _____

11. How would you rate the overall success of your assistance with regard to the target child's referral problem? (Check one.)

Dramatic improvement with all problems _____
Slight improvement, but major problems still remain _____
General worsening _____
Clear improvement, but some problems still remain _____
No change or any improvements were balanced by worsening prob-
    lems in other areas _____

Therapist Termination Report (Continued)

12. As a result of treatment, the child's behavior is:

    Worse   _____
    Unchanged   _____
    Somewhat better   _____
    Much better   _____
    Completely better   _____

13. How would you rate the effects (direct or carryover) of your assistance on the target child's emotional well-being (viz., self-image, happiness, self-confidence)? (Check one.)

    Worsening   _____
    No change   _____
    Slight improvement   _____
    Clear improvement   _____
    Dramatic improvement   _____

14. As a result of treatment, the child's attitude and feelings about him/herself are:

    Worse   _____
    Unchanged   _____
    Somewhat better   _____
    Much better   _____
    Completely better   _____

15. Compared to other children, how would you rate the target child's <u>current</u> behavior and social functioning? (Check one.)

    Much better, a "model" child   _____
    Better behaved   _____
    Average   _____
    Somewhat worse but not necessarily
       likely to stand out   _____
    Clearly worse   _____

16. How would you rate the effects (direct or carryover) of your assistance on the target child's siblings? (Check one.)

    No siblings   _____
    Siblings had so few problems or were
       so detached from family that it was
       impossible to assess impact   _____
    Dramatic improvement in sibling be-
       havior   _____
    Clear improvement, but some problems
       remain   _____
    Slight improvement, but major prob-
       lems remain   _____
    No change or any improvements were
       balanced by worsening problems in
       other areas   _____
    General worsening   _____

17. How would you rate the effects (direct or carryover) of your assistance on the mother's/father's parenting skills? (Check one.)

	Mother	Father
Dramatic improvement	_____	_____
Clear improvement, but some problems remain	_____	_____
Slight improvement, but major problems remain	_____	_____
No change	_____	_____
General worsening	_____	_____
This parent was absent	_____	_____

Therapist Termination Report (Continued)

18. As a result of treatment, the parents' (or parent's) ability to manage their child is:

Worse   _____
Unchanged   _____
Somewhat better   _____
Much better   _____
Completely better   _____

19. As a result of treatment, the parents' (or parent's) attitude toward their child is:

Worse   _____
Unchanged   _____
Somewhat better   _____
Much better   _____
Completely better   _____

20. How would you rate the effects (direct or carryover) of your assistance on the parent(s)' adult life adjustment (viz., employment, social functioning, economic functioning)? (Check one.)

	Mother	Father
This area was never a problem	_____	_____
Clear and dramatic improvement	_____	_____
Some improvement, but some problems remain	_____	_____
Slight improvement, but major problems remain	_____	_____
No change or any improvements were balanced by worsening problems in other areas	_____	_____
General worsening	_____	_____
This parent was absent	_____	_____

21. How would you rate the effects (direct or carryover) of your assistance on the parents' marital relationship? (Check one.)

Not applicable   _____
This area was never a problem   _____
Clear and dramatic improvement   _____
Some improvements, but some problems remain   _____
No change or any improvements were balanced by worsening problems in other areas   _____
General worsening   _____

22. In terms of problems within the family other than those involving the child's behavior, treatment had a:

Worsening effect   _____
No effect   _____
Minor positive effect   _____
Clearly positive effect   _____
Dramatically positive effect   _____

23. How likely is it that this child and/or family will need help in the future for problems similar to the target child's presenting problem? (Check one.)

Not likely at all   _____
Perhaps some minor assistance   _____
Probably some assistance   _____
Strong possibility of future need   _____
They still need assistance   _____

Therapist Termination Report (Continued)

24. The chances that this child will have serious behavior problems in the future are:

    Very likely   _____
    Likely   _____
    Unclear   _____
    Not too likely   _____
    Not likely at all   _____

25. Compared to other families with whom you have worked, how much did you like this family? (Check one.)

    A great deal   _____
    More   _____
    Average   _____
    Slightly less   _____
    Much less   _____

26. In comparison to similar children and families you have worked with, this family was:

    Much harder to help   _____
    Slightly harder to help   _____
    About averge   _____
    Easier to help   _____
    Much easier to help   _____

27. In applying the home-based program, I found it: (Check one.)

    A very useful approach for this family   _____
    Useful in resolving only some of the
       presenting problems   _____
    Not really useful with this family   _____

28. The treatment methods I used with this family appeared to have been:

    Not helpful at all   _____
    Unclear what else could have been tried   _____
    Fairly appropriate   _____
    Very appropriate   _____
    Exactly what they needed   _____

29. I would rate my adherence to the program as outlined in the clinical manual and taught during training and follow-up training sessions as: (Check one.)

    Very close adherence   _____
    Generally adhered, but made
    several changes   _____
    Selected parts of program, but
    used other approaches extensively   _____
    Used program only slightly   _____
    Did not use program   _____
    Explain if changes in program
    were made.   _____

Number of children:

At beginning of treatment	At end of treatment
In home _____	_____
Reunified _____	_____
In foster care _____	_____
Terminated _____	_____

On last page: Write a summary report of your therapy experiences with this family. Include presenting problem(s), topics covered, cooperation, and recommendations.

Post Parents Rating Form

Name: _____

Date: _____

Child: _____

Check one: Male parent/guardian _____
                    Female parent/guardian _____

Side effects of treatment

Directions: Please check ( ) and provide a brief description of all that apply.

Did treatment produce any underexpected benefits to:

1. (   ) You? Describe: _____

2. (   ) Your spouse? Describe: _____

3. (   ) Your marriage? Describe: _____

4. (   ) Another child besides the identified child? Describe: _____

5. (   ) Parent-child relations? Describe: _____

6. (   ) Sibling relations? Describe: _____

7. (   ) Child-peer relations? Describe: _____

8. (   ) Other? Describe: _____

Did treatment produce any negative side effects to:

9. (   ) You? Describe: _____

10. (   ) Your spouse? Describe: _____

11. (   ) Your marriage? Describe: _____

12. (   ) Another child besides the patient? Describe: _____

13. (   ) Parent-child relations? Describe: _____

14. (   ) Sibling relations? Describe: _____

15. (   ) Child-peer relations? Describe: _____

16. (   ) Other? Describe: _____

Post Parents Rating Form (Continued)

Directions: Briefly answer each of the next four questions.

17. What was the biggest change your child experienced while in treatment, if any? ____

_____

_____

18. What about treatment was most helpful to you, if anything? _____

_____

_____

19. What would you suggest to improve treatment, if anything? _____

_____

_____

20. Why did you stop treatment when you did? _____

_____

_____

Directions: Check or "X" the answer that is closest to your feelings about the services you have received.

21. The problems of my child that were treated are, at this time:

Worse	_____
The same	_____
Better	_____
Much better	_____
Very much better	_____

22. Because of the services our family received, my feelings about my child(ren) are:

Very much better	_____
Much better	_____
Better	_____
The same	_____
Worse	_____

23. Because of the services our family received, my family gets along:

Worse	_____
The same	_____
Better	_____
Much better	_____
Very much better	_____

24. Treating my child's problems in the home by using this type of family therapy program is:

Much worse than I thought it would be	_____
Not as good as I thought it would be	_____
About what I thought it would be	_____
A little better than I thought it would be	_____
Much better than I thought it would be	_____

25. How confident are you in managing current problems in the home on your own?

Not confident at all	_____
Sometimes confident	_____
About as confident as I thought I'd be	_____
Usually confident	_____
Very confident	_____

Post Parents Rating Form (Continued)

26. How frequently do you use the overall group of techniques discussed in the treatment (rewards, good communication, self-control, discipline methods, etc.)?

Never	_____
Sometimes	_____
Regularly	_____
More often than not	_____
Always	_____

27. My therapist/counselor seemed to care about my child and my problems:

Not at all	_____
A little	_____
Seems to care	_____
Really does care a lot	_____
Went out of their way for us	_____

28. The help I have gotten is:

Worse than I thought I'd get	_____
About what I thought I'd get	_____
A little better than I thought I'd get	_____
Much more than I thought I'd get	_____
A real surprise at how much help I got	_____

29. If I were talking to the people who give the money for these services, I would tell them:

Give it a lot more money to help many more families	_____
Give it more money than it's getting now	_____
They should keep paying for it	_____
Big changes should be made before more money gets spent	_____
Not to spend any more money on these services	_____

Appendix B

Common Problems Checklist

Common Problems Presented by Parents

---

1. My child started a fight with a brother or sister.
2. My child didn't help a brother or sister when needed.
3. My child played music or TV too loudly.
4. My child was late coming home.
5. My child didn't clean up.
6. My child interrupts conversations.
7. My child answered me rudely.
8. My child acted silly or fresh in front of company.
9. My child didn't listen to me.
10. My child left clothes lying around the house.
11. My child refuses to help around the house.
12. My child lied to me.
13. My child stole something.
14. My child used dirty words.
15. My child bothered me when I was on the phone.

Parent, write the problem you select here: _____

Common Problems Presented by Children

---

1. My parent played music or TV too loudly.
2. My parent was late coming home.
3. My parent forgot to buy something we needed.
4. My parent nagged me about eating dinner.
5. My parent bothered me when I was on the phone.
6. My parent intruded on me.
7. My parent criticized me in front of my friends.
8. My parent ignored my friends.
9. My parent nagged me about doing my homework.
10. My parent left clothing lying around the house.
11. My parent screamed at me.
12. My parent complained to me.
13. My parent wouldn't tuck me into bed.
14. My parent wouldn't get me a toy when I asked.
15. My parent was rude to my friends.

Child, write the problem you select here: _____

References

Achenbach, T., & Edelbrock, C. (1983). *Manual for the child behavior checklist and revised child behavior profile.* Burlington, VT: University of Vermont Department of Psychiatry.

Achenbach, T., & Edelbrock, C. (1986). *Manual for the teacher's report form and teacher version of the child behavior profile.* Burlington, VT: University of Vermont Department of Psychiatry.

Achenbach, T., & Edelbrock, C. (1987). *Manual for the youth self-report and profile.* Burlington, VT: University of Vermont Department of Psychiatry.

Achenbach, T., & McConaughy, S. (1987). *Empirically based assessment of child and adolescent psychopathology: Practical applications.* Newbury Park, CA: Sage Publications.

Achenbach, T., & McConaughy, S. (1989). *Semistructured clinical interview for children aged 6–11.* Burlington, VT: University of Vermont Department of Psychiatry.

Adams, P. R., & Adams, C. R. (1987). Intervention with runaway youth and their families: Theory and practice. In J. C. Coleman (Ed.), *Working with troubled adolescents: A handbook* (pp. 281–300). London: Academic Press.

Alexander, J., Barton, C., Schiavo, R., & Parsons, B. (1976). Systems-behavioral intervention with families of delinquents: Therapist characteristics, family behavior, and outcome. *Journal of Consulting and Clinical Psychology, 31,* 219–225.

American Psychiatric Association. (1987). *Diagnostic and statistical manual of mental disorders (3rd ed. rev.)* Washington, DC: Author.

Arnold, J., Levine, A., & Patterson, G. (1975). Changes in sibling behavior following family intervention. *Journal of Consulting and Clinical Psychology, 43,* 683–688.

Averill, J. R. (1983). Studies on anger and aggression: Implications for theories of emotion. *American Psychologist, 38,* 1145–1160.

Bahm, A., Chandler, C., & Eisenberg, L. (1961). *Diagnostic characteristics related to service of psychiatric clinics for children.* Paper presented at the 38th Annual Convention of Orthopsychiatry, Munich, Germany.

Bandura, A. (1969). *Principles of behavior modification.* Englewood Cliffs, NJ: Prentice-Hall.

Bandura, A. (1973). *Aggression: A social learning analysis.* Englewood Cliffs, NJ: Prentice-Hall.

Bandura, A. (1977). *Social learning theory.* Englewood Cliffs, NJ: Prentice-Hall.

Bandura, A. (1986). *Social foundations of thought and action.* Englewood Cliffs, NJ: Prentice-Hall.

Barker, R., Dembo, T., & Lewin, K. (Eds.). (1941). Frustration and regression: An experiment with young children. *University of Iowa Studies in Child Welfare, 1* (Whole No. 386).

Baum, C., & Forehand, R. (1981). Long term follow-up assessment of parent training by use of multiple outcome measures. *Behavior Therapy, 12,* 643–652.

Beck, A. (1967). *Depression: Clinical, experimental, and theoretical aspects.* New York: Harper & Row.

Beck, A. (1972). *Depression: Causes and treatment.* Philadelphia: University of Pennsylvania.

Berkowitz, L. (1962). *Aggression: A social psychological anaylsis.* New York: McGraw-Hill.

Berkowitz, L. (1965). The concept of aggressive drive: Some additional considerations. In L. Berkowitz (Ed.), *Advances in experimental social psychology* (pp. 301–329). New York: Academic Press.

Berkowitz, L. (1969). The frustration-aggression hypothesis revisited. In L. Berkowitz (Ed.), *Roots of aggression: A reexamination of the frustration-aggression hypothesis* (pp. 1–28). New York: Atherton Press.

Berkowitz, L. (1970). The contagion of violence: An S-R mediational analysis of some effects of observed aggression. In W. J. Arnold & M. M. Page (Eds.), *Nebraska symposium on motivation* (pp. 95–135). Lincoln, NE: University of Nebraska.

Berkowitz, L. (1973). Control of aggression. In B. M. Caldwell & R. Riecute (Eds.), *Review of child development research* (pp. 95–140). Chicago: University of Chicago Press.

Berkowitz, L. (1974). Some determinants of impulsive aggression: Role of mediated associations with reinforcement for aggression. *Psychological Review, 81,* 165–176.

Bernal, M., Klinnert, M., & Schultz, L. (1980). Outcome evaluation of behavioral parent training and client-centered parent counseling for children with conduct problems. *Journal of Applied Behavior Analysis, 13,* 677–691.

Birchler, G. (1988). Handling resistance to change. In I. Falloon (Ed.), *Handbook of behavioral family therapy* (pp. 128–155). New York: Guilford Publications.

Blechman, E. (1985). *Solving child behavior problems at home and at school.* Champaign, IL: Research Press.

Bolstad, O., & Johnson, S. (1972). Self-regulation in the modification of disruptive classroom behavior. *Journal of Applied Behavior Analysis, 5,* 443–454.

Boyer, M., & Horne, A. M. (1988). *Family therapy with multiproblem families.* Paper presented at the Annual Conference of the Indiana Association for Counseling and Development, Indianapolis, IN.

Burgess, R. (1978). Child abuse: A social-interactional analysis. In B. Lahey & A. Kazdin (Eds.), *Advances in clinical child psychology* (Vol. 2, pp. 143–172). New York: Plenum Press.

Burgess, R., & Richardson, R. (1984). Coercive interpersonal contingencies as determinants of child abuse: Implications for treatment and prevention. In R. F. Dangel & R. A. Polster (Eds.), *Behavioral parent training: Issues in research and practice* (pp. 239–259). New York: Guilford Publications.

Cairns, R. B. (1979a). *The analysis of social interactions: Methods, issues and illustrations.* Hillsdale, NJ: Lawrence Erlbaum Associates.

Cairns, R. B. (1979b). *Social development: The origins and plasticity of interchanges.* San Franciso: W H Freeman.

Cairns, R. B. (1979c). *Social development: The origins and plasticity of interchanges.* San Francisco: W H Freeman.

Camp, B., Blom, H., & van Doorninck, W. (1977). Think aloud: A program for developing self-control in young aggressive boys. *Journal of Abnormal Child Psychology, 5,* 157–168.

Carlson, G. A., & Cantwell, D. P. (1980). A survey of depressive symptoms, syndrome and disorder in a child psychiatric population. *Journal of Child Psychology and Psychiatry, 21,* 19–25.

Cole, J., Dodge, K., & Coppotelli, H. (1982). Dimensions and types of social status: Across-age perspective. *Developmental Psychology, 18,* 557–570.

Derogatis, L. R. (1983). *SCL-90-R administration, scoring, and procedures manual — II.* Towson, MD: Clinical Psychometric Research.

Dinkmeyer, D., & McKay, G. D. (1976). *Systematic training for effective parenting.* Circle Pines, MN: American Guidance Service.

Dinkmeyer, D., & McKay, G. D. (1982). *The parent's handbook: Systematic training for effective parenting.* Circle Pines, MN: American Guidance Service.

Dodge, K. A. (1980). Social cognition and children's aggressive behavior. *Child Development, 51,* 162–170.

Dollard, J., Doob, L. W., Miller, N. E., Mowrer, O. H., & Sears, R. R. (1939). *Frustration and aggression.* New Haven, CT: Yale University Press.

Downing, C. J. (1983). A positive way to help families. *Elementary School Guidance and Counseling, 17,* 208–213.

Ekehammar, B. (1974). Interactionism in personality from a historical perspective. *Psychological Bulletin, 81,* 1026–1048.

Ellis, A. (in press). Rational-emotive family therapy. In A. M. Horne, & J. L. Passmore (Eds.), *Family counseling and therapy* (2nd ed.). Itasca, IL: F E Peacock.

Eron, L. D. (1980). Prescription for reduction of aggression. *American Psychologist, 35,* 244–252.

Eyberg, S., & Johnson, S. (1974). Multiple assessment of behavior modification with families: Effects of contingency contracting and order of treated problems. *Journal of Consulting and Clinical Psychology, 42,* 594–606.

Fawl, C. L. (1963). Disturbances experienced by children in their natural habitats. In R. Baker (Ed.), *The stream of behavior* (pp. 99–126). New York: Appleton-Century-Crofts.

Feshbach, S. (1964). The function of aggression and the regulation of aggressive drive. *Psychological Review, 71,* 257–272.

Feshbach, S. (1970). Aggression. In P. H. Mussen (Ed.), *Carmichael's manual of child psychology* (pp. 159–259). New York: John Wiley & Sons.

Flanagan, J. (1954). The critical incident technique. *Psychological Bulletin, 51,* 327–358.

Fleischman, M. (1981). A replication of Patterson's "Intervention for boys with conduct problems." *Journal of Consulting and Clinical Psychology, 49,* 342–351.

Fleischman, M., & Horne, A. (1979). Working with families: A social learning approach. *Contemporary Education, 50,* 66–71.

Fleischman, M., Horne, A., & Arthur, J. (1983). *Troubled families: A treatment program.* Champaign, IL: Research Press.

Forehand, R., Furey, W., & McMahon, R. (1984). The role of maternal distress in a parent training program to modify child non-compliance. *Behavior Research and Therapy, 12,* 415–421.

Forehand, R., & King, H. (1974). Pre-school children's non-compliance: Effects of short-term behavior therapy. *Journal of Community Psychology, 2,* 22–42.

Forehand, R., & King, H. (1977). Noncompliant children: Effects of parent training on behavior and attitude change. *Behavior Modification, 1,* 93–108.

Forehand, R., Long, N., Brody, G., & Fauber, R. (1985). *Home predictors of young adolescents' school behavior and academic performance.* Manuscript submitted for publication.

Forehand, R., & McMahon, R. (1981). *Helping the noncompliant child: A clinician's guide to parent training.* New York: Guilford Publications.

Forehand, R., Sturgis, E., McMahon, R., Aguar, D., Green, K., Wells, K., & Breiner, J. (1979). Parent behavioral training to modify child non-compliance: Treatment generalization across time and from home to school. *Behavior Modification, 3,* 3–25.

Forehand, R., Wells, K., McMahon, R., & Griest, D. (1982). Side effects of parent counseling on marital satisfaction. *Journal of Counseling Psychology, 29,* 104–107.

Foster, S., Prinz, R., & O'Leary, D. (1983). Impact of problem-solving communication training and generalization procedures on family conflict. *Child and Family Behavior Therapy, 5,* 1–23.

Freud, S. (1920). *A general introduction to psychoanalysis.* New York: Boni and Liveright.

Freud, S. (1959). *Beyond the pleasure principle.* New York: Bantam Books.

Fuelle, J. (1981). *Differences in cognitive styles of mothers of impulsive and reflective children.* Unpublished doctoral dissertation, Indiana State University, Terre Haute, IN.

Gersten, J. C., Langner, T. S., Eisenberg, J. G., Simcha-Fagan, O., & McCarthy, E. (1976). Stability and change in types of behavioral distrubances of children and adolescents. *Journal of Abnormal Child Psychology, 4,* 111–127.

Gillespie, W. H. (1971). Aggression and instinct theory. *International Journal of Psychoanalysis, 52,* 155–160.

Gittelman, R., & Kanner, A. (1986). Psycho-pharmaco-therapy. In H. Quay & J. Werry (Eds.), *Psychopathological disorders of childhood* (3rd ed., pp. 455–494). New York: John Wiley & Sons.

Glaser, B. A. (1989). *A bidirectional study of functional, distressed, and abusive families.* Unpublished doctoral dissertation, Indiana State University, Terre Haute, IN.

Glasser, W. (1972). *Reality therapy.* New York: Harper & Row.

Goldman, J., Stein, C., & Guerry, S. (1983). *Psychological methods of child assessment.* New York: Brunner/Mazel.

Goodenough, F. L. (1933). *Anger in young children.* Minneapolis: University of Minnesota Press.

Gordon, T. (1970). *Parent effectiveness training: The "no-lose" program for raising responsible children.* New York: Peter Wyden.

Gottman, J., Notarius, C., Gonso, J., & Markman, H. (1976). *A couples' guide to communication.* Champaign, IL: Research Press.

Griest, D., Forehand, R., Wells, K., & McMahon, R. (1980). An examination of differences between nonclinic and behavior problem clinic-referred children and their mothers. *Journal of Abnormal Psychology, 89,* 497–500.

Griest, D., & Wells, K. (1983). Behavioral family therapy with conduct disorders in children. *Behavior Therapy, 14,* 37–53.

Gross, A. (1983). Conduct disorders. In M. Hersen (Ed.), *Outpatient behavior therapy: A clinical guide* (pp. 307–322). New York: Grune & Stratton.

Haubold, L. (1989). *A comparison of social cognitions of aggressive and model boys.* Unpublished doctoral dissertation, Indiana State University, Terre Haute, IN.

Hoghughi, M., Lyons, J., Muckley, A., & Swainston, M. (1988). *Treating problem children: Issues, methods and practice.* London: Sage Publications.

Horne, A. M. (1981). Aggressive behavior in normal and deviant members of intact versus mother-only families. *Journal of Abnormal Child Psychology, 9,* 283–290.

Horne, A. M. (1982). Counseling families: Social learning family therapy. In A. M. Horne & M. M. Ohlsen (Eds.), *Family counseling and therapy* (pp. 360–388). Itasca, IL: F E Peacock.

Horne, A. M. (1989). *Therapist termination report.* Unpublished document. Athens, GA: The University of Georgia.

Horne, A. M., Boyer, M., Sayger, T. V., & Passmore, J. L. (1988, October). *Applications of social learning family therapy with multi-problem families.* Program presented at the 46th Annual Conference of the American Association for Marriage and Family Therapy, New Orleans.

Horne, A. M., & Fuelle, J. (1981). *Problem-solving interactional patterns of impulsive and reflective children and their mothers.* Paper presented at the 15th Annual Convention of the Association for the Advancement of Behavior Therapy, Toronto.

Horne, A. M., & Patterson, G. (1980). Working with parents of aggressive children. In R. Abidin (Ed.), *Parent education handbook* (pp. 159–184). Springfield, IL: Charles C Thomas.

Horne, A. M. & Sayger, T. V. (1989a). *Factors contributing to change scale.* Unpublished document. Athens, GA: The University of Georgia.

Horne, A. M., & Sayger, T. V. (1989b). *Parent rating form.* Unpublished document. Athens, GA: The University of Georgia.

Horne, A. M., & Van Dyck, B. (1983). Treatment and maintenance of social learning family therapy. *Behavior Therapy, 14,* 606–613.

Humphreys, L., Forehand, R., McMahon, R., & Roberts, M. (1978). Parent behavioral training to modify child noncompliance: Effects on untreated siblings. *Journal of Behavior Therapy and Experimental Psychiatry, 9,* 235–238.

Jacobson, N., & Margolin, G. (1979). *Marital therapy: Strategies based on social learning and behavior exchange principles.* New York: Brunner/Mazel.

James, L. C. (1987). *A study of the differences in touch patterns between functional and dysfunctional families.* Unpublished doctoral dissertation, Indiana State University, Terre Haute, IN.

Johnson, S., & Christensen, A. (1975). Multiple criterion follow-up of behavior modification with families. *Jounal of Abnormal Child Psychology, 3,* 135–154.

Johnson, S., & Lobitz, G. (1974). The personal and marital adjustment of parents as related to observed child deviance and parenting behaviors. *Journal of Abnormal Child Psychology, 2,* 192–207.

Jones, D. W. (1987). Recent developments in work with young offenders. In J. C. Coleman (Ed.), *working with troubled adolescents: A handbook* (pp. 265–280). London: Academic Press.

Kazdin, A. E. (1987). *Conduct disorders in childhood and adolescence.* Newbury Park, CA: Sage Publications.

Kazdin, A. E. (1988). *Child psychotherapy: Developing and identifying effective treatments.* New York: Pergamon Press.

Kazdin, A. E., Esveldt-Dawson, K., French, N. H., & Unis, A. S. (1987). Problem-solving skills training and relationship therapy in the treatment of antisocial child behavior. *Journal of Consulting and Clinical Psychology, 55,* 76–85.

Keat, D. B. (1979). *Multimodel therapy with children.* New York: Pergamon Press.

Kelly, J. (1983). *Treating child abusive families: Intervention based on skills training principles.* New York: Plenum Press.

Kendall, P., & Braswell, L. (1985). *Cognitive-behavioral therapy for impulsive children.* New York: Guilford Publications.

Kendall, P., & Hollon, S. (1979). *Cognitive-behavioral interventions: Theory, research and procedures.* New York: Academic Press.

Kirby, E., & Grimley, L. (1986). *Understanding and treating attention deficit disorder.* New York: Pergamon Press.

Kniskern, D., & Gurman, A. (1981). Advances and prospects in family therapy research. In J. P. Vincent (Ed.), *Advances in family intervention, assessment, and theory* (Vol. 2, pp. 215–239). Greenwich, CT: JAI Press.

Knutson, J. F. (1978). Child abuse as an area of aggression research. *Journal of Pediatric Psychology, 3,* 20–27.

Kolko, D., & Kazdin, A. (1986). A conceptualization of firesetting in children and adolescents. *Journal of Abnormal Child Psychology, 14,* 49–61.

Kolko, D., & Kazdin, A. (1988). Prevalence of firesetting and related behaviors among child psychiatric patients. *Journal of Consulting and Clinical Psychology, 56,* 628–630.

Kolko, D., Kazdin, A., & Meyer, E. (1985). Aggression and psychopathology in childhood firesetters: Parent and child reports. *Journal of Consulting and Clinical Psychology, 53,* 377–385.

Kovacs, M. (1981). Rating scales to assess depression in school-aged children. *Acta Pae-dopsychiatrica, 46,* 305–315.

Lahey, B., Conger, R., Atkeson, B., & Teiber, F. (1984). Parenting behavior and emotional status of physically abusive mothers. *Journal of Consulting and Clinical Psychology, 52,* 1062–1071.

Last, C., Griest, D., & Kazdin, A. (1985). Physiological and cognitive assessment of a fire-setting child. *Behavior Modification, 9,* 94–102.

Lederer, W., & Jackson, D. (1968). *Mirages of marriage.* New York: W W Norton.

Levitt, E. (1971). Research on psychotherapy with children. In A. Bergin & S. Garfield (Eds.), *Handbook of psychotherapy and behavior change* (pp. 474–494). New York: John Wiley & Sons.

Lewis, J., Beavers, W., Gossett, J., & Phillips, V. (1976). *No single thread: Psychological health in family systems.* New York: Brunner/Mazel.

Liberman, R., Wheeler, E., & Sanders, N. (1976). Behavioral therapy for marital dishar-mony: An educational approach. *Journal of Marriage and Family Counseling, 2,* 383–395.

Little, V., & Kendall, P. (1979). Cognitive-behavioral intervention with delinquents: Prob-lem-solving, role-taking, and self-control. In P. Kendall & S. Hollon (Eds.), *Cognitive-behavioral interventions: Theory, research, and practice.* New York: Academic Press.

Littman, D., & Patterson, G. R. (1980). *Unpredictable aggression: A common dilemma.* Un-published manuscript, Oregon Social Learning Center, Eugene, OR.

Lobitz, G., & Johnson, S. (1975). Normal versus deviant children: A multimethod com-parison. *Journal of Abnormal Child Psychology, 3,* 353–374.

Lochman, J. E. (1987). Self- and peer perceptions and attributional biases of aggressive and non-aggressive boys in dyadic interactions. *Journal of Consulting and Clinical Psy-chology, 55,* 404–410.

Locke, H., & Wallace, K. (1959). Short marital-adjustment and prediction tests: Their reliability and validity. *Marriage and Family Living, 21,* 251–255.

Lorber, R., Felton, D., & Reid, J. (1984). A social learning approach to the reduction of coercive processes in child abusive families: A molecular analysis. *Advances in Behavior Research and Therapy, 6,* 29–45.

Lorber, R., & Patterson, G. R. (1981). The aggressive child: A concomitant of a coercive system. In J. P. Vincent (Ed.), *Advances in family intervention, assessment, and theory* (Vol. 2, pp. 47–87). Greenwich, CT: JAI Press.

Lorenz, K. Z. (1964). Ritualized fighting. In J. D. Carthy & F. J. Ebling (Eds.), *The natural history of aggression* (pp. 39–50). New York: Academic Press.

Lorenz, K. Z. (1966). *On aggression.* New York: Harcourt Brace Jovanovich.

Lowe, R. (1982). Adlerian/Dreikursian family counseling. In A. M. Horne & M. M. Ohlsen (Eds.), *Family Counseling and Therapy* (pp. 329–359). Itasca, IL: F E Peacock.

MacMillan, D., & Kavale, K. (1986). Educational intervention. In H. Quay & J. Werry (Eds.), *Psychopathological disorders of childhood* (3rd ed., pp. 583–621). New York: John Wiley & Sons.

Maier, N. R. F. (1949). *Frustration: The study of behavior without a goal.* New York: McGraw-Hill.

Martin, R. (1988). *Assessment of personality and behavior problems.* New York: Guilford Pub-lications.

McAuley, R. (1982). Training parents to modify conduct problems in their children. *Journal of Child Psychology and Psychiatry and Allied Disciplines, 23,* 335–342.

McCauley, R. (1988). Parent training: Clinical applications. In I. Falloon (Ed.), *Handbook of behavioral family therapy* (pp. 160–180. New York: Guilford Publications.

McMahon, R., & Forehand, R. (1984). Parent training for the noncompliant child: Treatment outcome, generalization, and adjunctive therapy procedures. In R. Dangel & R. Polster (Eds.), *Parent training* (pp. 298–328). New York: Guilford Publications.

McMahon, R., Forehand, R., & Griest, D. (1981). Effects of knowledge of social learning principles on enhancing treatment outcome and generalization in a parent training program. *Journal of Consulting and Clinical Psychology, 49,* 526–532.

Mednick, S. A., & Christiansen, K.O. (1977). *Biosocial bases of criminal behavior.* New York: Gardner Press.

Mednick, S. A., & Hutchings, B. (1977). Criminality in adoptees and their adoptive and biological parents: A pilot study. In S. A. Mednick & K. O. Christiansen (Eds.), *Biosocial bases of criminal behavior.* New York: Gardner Press.

Megargee, E. I., & Hokanson, J. E. (1970). Theoretical formulations. In E. I. Megargee & J. E. Hokanson (Eds.), *The dynamics of aggression* (pp. 1–4). New York: Harper & Row.

Melnick, B., & Hurley, J. B. (1969). Distinctive personality attributes of child-abusing mothers. *Journal of Consulting and Clinical Psychology, 33,* 746–749.

Meltzoff, J., & Kornreich, M. (1970). *Research in psychotherapy.* New York: Atherton Press.

Miller, N. E. (1941). The frustration-aggression hypothesis. *Psychological Review, 48,* 337–342.

Miller, N. E. (1948). Theory and experiment relating psychoanalytic displacement to stimulus-response generalization. *Journal of Abnormal and Social Psychology, 43,* 155–178.

Moos, R. H. (1974). *Preliminary manual for family, work, and group environment scales.* Palo Alto, CA: Consulting Psychologists.

Moos, R. H., & Moos, B. S. (1984). *Family environment scale manual.* Palo Alto, CA: Consulting Psychologists.

Moreland, J., Schwebel, A., Beck, S., & Wells, R. (1982). Parents as therapists: A review of the behavior therapy parent training literature, 1975–1981. *Behavior Modification, 6,* 250–276.

Morris, P. W., Horne, A. M., Jessell, J. C., Passmore, J. L., Walker, J. M., & Sayger, T. V. (1988). Behavioral and cognitive characteristics of fathers of aggressive and well-behaved boys. *Journal of Cognitive Psychotherapy: An International Quarterly, 2,* 251–265.

Morris, S., Alexander, J., & Waldron, H. (1988). Functional family therapy. In I. Falloon (Ed.), *Handbook of behavioral family therapy* (pp. 107–127). New York: Guilford Publications.

Nickerson, M., Light, R., Blechman, E., & Gandelman, B. (Eds.). (1976, Winter). Three measures of problem solving behavior: A procedural manual. *JSAS Catalog of Selected Documents in Psychology* (Ms. No. 1190).

O'Dell, S. (1974). Training parents in behavior modification: A review. *Psychological Bulletin, 81,* 418–433.

Oates, M. R. (1979). A classification of child abuse and its relation to treatment and prognosis. *Child Abuse and Neglect, 3,* 907–915.

Ohlsen, M., Horne, A., & Lawe, C. (1988). *Group counseling* (3rd ed.). New York: Holt, Rinehart, & Winston.

Ollendick, T., & Hersen, M. (1984). *Child behavior assessment.* New York: Pergamon Press.

Olson, D., Russell, C., & Sprenkle, D. (1980). Marital and family therapy: A decade review. *Journal of Marriage and Family Therapy, 42,* 973–993.

Olweus, D. (1976). *Longitudional studies of aggressive reaction patterns: A review.* Paper presented at the 21st International Congress of Psychology, Paris.

Olweus, D. (1979). Stability of aggressive reaction patterns in males: A review. *Psychological Bulletin, 86,* 852–875.

Otto, M. L., & Smith, D. G. (1980). Child abuse: A cognitive behavioral intervention model. *Journal of Marital and Family Therapy, 6,* 425–430.

Patterson, G. (1974). Interventions for boys with conduct problems: Multiple settings, treatments, and criteria. *Journal of Consulting and Clinical Psychology, 42,* 471–481.

Patterson, G. (1975). Multiple evaluations of a parent training program. In T. Tompson, & W. S. Dockens, III (Eds.), *Applications of behavior modification* (pp. 299–322). New York: Academic Press.

Patterson, G. (1980). Mothers: The unacknowledged victims. *Monographs of the Society for Research in Child Development, 45*(5), 1–64. (Serial No. 186)

Patterson, G. (1982). *Coercive family process.* Eugene, OR: Castalia.

Patterson, G. (1986). Performance models for antisocial boys. *American Psychologist, 41,* 432–444.

Patterson, G., & Hops, H. (1972). Coercion, a game for two: Intervention techniques for marital conflict. In R. Ulrich, & P. Mountjoy (Eds.), *The experimental analysis of social behavior* (pp. 424–440). New York: Appleton-Century-Crofts.

Patterson, G., Ray, R., Shaw, D., & Cobb, J. (1969). *Manual for coding of family interactions* (rev. ed.). New York: Microfiche Publications.

Patterson, G., & Reid, J. (1973). Intervention for families of aggressive boys: A replication study. *Behavior Research and Therapy, 11,* 383–394.

Patterson, G., & Reid, J. (1984). Some interactional processes within the family: The study of the moment-by-moment family transactions in which human social development is imbedded. *Journal of Applied Developmental Psychology, 5,* 237–262.

Patterson, G., Reid, J., Jones, R., & Conger, R. (1975). *A social learning approach to family intervention. Vol. I: Families with aggressive children.* Eugene, OR: Castalia.

Patterson, G., Reid, J., & Maerov, S. (1978). The observational system: Methodological issues and psychometric properties. In J. Reid (Ed.), *A social learning approach to family intervention, Vol. 2: Observations in the home setting* (pp. 11–19). Eugene, OR: Castalia.

Peed, S., Roberts, M., & Forehand, R. (1977). Evaluation of the effectiveness of a standardized parent training program in altering the interaction of mothers and their noncompliant children. *Behavior Modification, 1,* 323–350.

Peryea, K. R. (1989). *Theoretical approaches to treatment of antisocial children with discussion specific to the juvenile justice system and public schools.* Unpublished master's project, Washington State University, Pullman, WA.

Pino, C., Simons, N., & Slawinowski, M. J. (1983). Development and application of the children's version of the family environment scale. *Journal of Mental Imagery, 7,* 75–82.

Pino, C., Simons, N., & Slawinowski, M. J. (1984). *The children's version of the family environment scale manual.* East Aurora, NY: Slosson Educational Publications.

Premack, D. (1959). Toward empirical behavior laws: 1. Positive reinforcement. *Psychological Review, 66,* 219–233.

Prinz, R., Conner, P., & Wilson, C. (1981). Hyperactive and aggressive behaviors in childhood: Interwined dimensions. *Journal of Abnormal Child Psychology, 9,* 287–295.

Quay, H. (1986a). Conduct disorders. In H. Quay & J. Werry (Eds.), *Psychopathological disorders of childhood* (pp. 35–72). New York: John Wiley & Sons.

Quay, H. (1986b). Residential treatment. In H. Quay & J. Werry (Eds.), *Psychopathological disorders of childhood* (pp. 558–582). New York: John Wiley & Sons.

Reeves, J. C., Werry, J. S., Elkind, G. S., & Zametkin, A. (1987). Attention deficit, conduct, oppositional, and anxiety disorders in children: II. Clinical characteristics. *Journal of the American Academy of Child and Adolescent Psychiatry, 26*(2), 144–155.

Reid, H. A. (1989). *Social learning therapy for families with aggressive boys: Individual family versus parent-group treatment.* Unpublished doctoral dissertation, Indiana State University, Terre Haute, IN.

Reid, J. B. (Ed.). (1978). *A social learning approach to family intervention. Vol. 2: Observation in home settings.* Eugene, OR: Castalia.

Reid, J. B., & Hendricks, A. (1973). A preliminary analysis of the effectiveness of direct home intervention for treatment of predelinquent boys who steal. In L. Hamerlynck, L. Handy, & E. Mash (Eds.), *Behavior therapy: Methodology, concepts, and practice.* Champaign, IL: Research Press.

Reid, J. B., & Patterson, G. (1976). The modification of aggression and stealing behavior of boys in the home setting. In A. Bandura, & E. Ribes (Eds.), *Experimental analyses of aggression and delinquency.* Hillsdale, NJ: Lawrence Erlbaum Associates.

Reid, J. B., Taplin, P., & Lorber, R. (1981). A social interactional approach to the treatment of abusive families. In R. Stuart (Ed.), *Violent behavior: Social learning approaches to prediction, management, and treatment* (pp. 83–101). New York: Brunner/Mazel.

Roach, J. (1958). Some social psychological characteristics of child guidance caseloads. *Journal of Consulting Psychology, 22,* 183–186.

Robins, N. L. (1966). *Deviant children grown up: A sociological and psychiatric study of sociopathic personality.* Baltimore, MD: Williams & Wilkins.

Sakheim, G., Vigdor, M., Gordon, M., & Helprin, L. (1985). A psychological profile of juvenile firesetters in residiential treatment. *Child Welfare, 64,* 453–476.

Sayger, T. V. (1987). The maintenance of treatment effects for families of aggressive boys participating in social learning family therapy. *Dissertation Abstracts International, 47*(09), 3318-A.

Sayger, T. V., Horne, A. M., & Glaser, B. (1989). *Side-effects of family therapy for child behavior problems on marital satisfaction.* Manuscript submitted for publication.

Sayger, T. V., Horne, A. M., Passmore, J. L., & Walker, J. M. (1988). Social learning family therapy with aggresive children: Treatment outcome and maintenance. *Journal of Family Psychology, 1*(3), 261–285.

Sayger, T. V., Horne, A. M., & Walker, J. M. (1987). Behavioral systems family counseling: A treatment program for families with disruptive children. *Contemporary Education, 58,* 160–166.

Sayger, T. V., & Szykula, S. A. (1987, May). *The side effects survey: Assessing the iatrogenic effects of child-focused therapy.* Paper presented at the Annual Conference of the Utah Psychololgical Association, Salt Lake City, UT.

Sayger, T. V., Szykula, S. A., Sudweeks, C., Morris, S. B., & Child, W. (1987, November). *The side-effects of participation in child-focused behavioral and strategic family therapies in an outpatient psychiatric facility.* Paper presented at the 21st Annual Convention of the Association for Advancement of Behavior Therapy, Boston.

Schaefer, C. E., Briesmeister, J. M., & Fitton, M. E. (1986). *Family therapy techniques for problem behaviors of children and teenagers.* San Francisco: Jossey-Bass.

Schneider, M., & Robin, A. (1976). The turtle technique: A method for the self-control of impulsive behavior. In J. Krumboltz, & C. Thoreson (Eds.), *Counseling methods* (pp. 157–162). New York: Holt, Rinehart, and Winston.

Scott, J. P. (1958). *Aggression.* Chicago: University of Chicago Press.

Sears, R. R., Whiting, J. W. M., Nowlis, V., & Sears, P. S. (1953). Some child-rearing antecendents of aggression and dependency in young children. *Genetic Psychology Monographs, 47,* 135–234.

Silberman, M. L., & Wheelan, S. A. (1980). *How to discipline without feeling guilty: Assertive relationships with children.* Champaign, IL: Research Press.

Sloane, M. P., & Meier, J. H. (1983). Typology for parents of abused children. *Child Abuse and Neglect, 7,* 443–450.

Spanier, G. B. (1979). The measurement of marital quality. *Journal of Sex and Marital Therapy, 5,* 288–300.

Spanier, G. B., & Thompson, L. (1982). A confirmatory analysis of the dyadic adjustment scale. *Journal of Marriage and the Family, 44,* 731–738.

Spivack, G., Platt, J., & Shure, M. (1976). *The problem-solving approach to adjustment.* San Fancisco: Jossey-Bass.

Stuart, R. (1980). *Helping couples change.* New York: Guilford Publications.

Szykula, S. A., Mas, C. H., Turner, C. W., Crowley, J., & Sayger, T. V. (1989). *Maternal social support and prosocial mother-child interactions.* Manuscript submitted for publication.

Szykula, S. A., Sayger, T. V., Morris, S. B., & Sudweeks, C. (1987). Child-focused behavior and strategic therapies: Outcome comparisons. *Psychotherapy: Theory, Research, Practice and Training, 24*(3S), 546–551.

Teuber, H., & Powers, E. (1953). Evaluating therapy in a delinquency prevention program. *Psychiatric Treatment, 21,* 138–147.

Todd, T., & Stanton, M. (1983). Research on marital and family therapy: Answers, issues, and recommendations for the futrue. In B. Wolman, & G. Stricker (Eds.), *Handbook of family and marital therapy* (pp. 91–115). New York: Plenum Press.

Van Valkenburg, M. C. (1986). Predictors of reduction of aggressive behavior of young boys. *Dissertation Abstracts International, 47*(02), 808-B.

Vasta, R. (1982). Physical child abuse: A dual-componet analysis. *Developmental Review, 2,* 125–149.

Wahler, R. (1980). The insular mother: Her problems in parent-child tratment. *Journal of Applied Behavior Anaylsis, 13,* 207–219.

Wahler, R., & Afton, A. (1980). Attentional processes in insular and noninsular mothers: Some differences in their summary reports about child problem behaviors. *Child Behavior Therapy, 2,* 25–41.

Walker, J. M. (1985). A study of the effectiveness of social learning family therapy for reducing aggressive behavior in boys. *Dissertation Abstracts International, 45*(09), 3088-B.

Walter, H., & Gilmore, S. (1973). Placebo versus social learning effects in parent training procedures designed to alter the behavior of aggressive boys. *Behavior Therapy, 4,* 361–377.

Wells, K. C. (1981). Assessment of children in outpatient settings. In M. Hersen, & A. Bellack (Eds.), *Behavioral assessment: A practical handbook* (pp. 484–533). New York: Pergamon Press.

Wells, K. C., & Forehand, R. (1985). Conduct and oppositional disorders. In P. H. Bornstein, & A. E. Kazdin (Eds.), *Handbook of clinical behavior therapy with children* (pp. 218–265). Homewood, IL: The Dorsey Press.

Wells, K. C., Forehand, R., & Griest, D. (1980). Generality of treatment effects from treated to untreated behaviors resulting from a parent training program. *Journal of Clinical Child Psychology, 8,* 217–219.

Wells, K. C., Griest, D., & Forehand, R. (1980). The use of a self-control package to enhance temporal generality of a parent training program. *Behavior Research and Therapy, 18,* 347–358.

Werry, J. S., Reeves, J. C., & Elkind, G. S. (1987). Attention deficit, conduct, oppositional, and anxiety disorders in children: A review of research on differentiating characteristics. *Journal of the American Academy of Child and Adolescent Psychiatry, 26*(2), 133–143.

Whalen, A., Jessell, J. C., & Horne, A. M. (1989). *Cognitions of mothers in families with aggressive and with well behaved choldren.* Unpublished study, Indiana State University, Terre Haute, IN.

Whiting, J. W. M., & Child, I. L. (1953). *Child training and personality.* New Haven, CT: Yale University.

Wiltz, N., & Patterson, G. (1974). An evaluation of parent training procedures designed to alter inappropriate aggressive behavior of boys. *Behavior Therapy, 5,* 215–221.

Wolfe, D. A. (1985). Child-abusive parents: An empirical review and analysis. *Psychological Bulletin, 97,* 462–482.

Wolfe, D. A., Kaufman, K., Aragona, J., & Sandler, J. (1981). *The child management program for abusive parents.* Winter Park, FL: Anna.

Wolfe, D. A., & Mosk, M. (1983). Behavioral comparisons of children from abusive and distressed families. *Journal of Consulting and Clinical Psychology, 51,* 702–708.

Wolfe, D. A., & Sandler, J. (1981). Training abusive parents in effective child management. *Behavior Modification, 5,* 320–335.

Yalom, I. (1985). *Theory and practice of group psychotherapy* (3rd ed). New York: Basic Books.

Zillman, D. (1979). *Hostility and aggression.* Hillsdale, NJ: Lawrence Erlbaum Associates.

Author Index

Subject Index

About the Authors

Arthur M. Horne (PhD, Southern Illinois University) is Professor and Director of Training in Counseling Psychology at the University of Georgia. Prior to his appointment there, Dr. Horne was at Indiana State University from 1971–1989, where he directed the Counseling Psychology program and, in 1979, began the Family Therapy Research Project (FTRP). The FTRP treated aggressive children through a family and school approach and included school- and clinic-based as well as home-based interventions. He is the coauthor of *Group Counseling* and *Troubled Families: A Treatment Program*, and coeditor of *Family Counseling and Therapy*.

Thomas V. Sayger (PhD, Indiana State University) is Assistant Professor at the University of Wisconsin-Madison. Dr. Sayger's primary responsibilities are in the university's master's program in counselor education and the APA-accredited doctoral training program in Counseling Psychology. Prior to his academic appointment at UW-Madison, Dr. Sayger was Assistant Professor at Washington State University. Dr. Sayger's published research has focused on family counseling with conduct- and oppositional-defiant-disordered children. His latest publications have appeared in the *Journal of Family Psychology, Psychotherapy*, and the *Journal of Cognitive Psychotherapy*. Dr. Sayger's clinical experiences include Director of the Family Therapy Research Project at Indiana State University, Chief Psychology Intern at Primary Children's Medical Center in Salt Lake City, and Counseling Assistant at the Washington State University Counseling Services Center. Dr. Sayger has conducted numerous conference workshops and received the 1986 Student Research Award for his research in the area of family therapy with aggressive children from Division 12 (Clinical Psychology), Section 1 (Clinical Child Psychology) of the American Psychological Association.

Psychology Practitioner Guidebooks

Editors

Arnold P. Goldstein, Syracuse University
Leonard Krasner, Stanford University & SUNY at Stony Brook
Sol L. Garfield, Washington University in St. Louis

William L. Golden, E. Thomas Dowd & Fred Friedberg—
HYPNOTHERAPY: A Modern Approach

Patricia Lacks—BEHAVIORAL TREATMENT FOR PERSISTENT INSOMNIA

Arnold P. Goldstein & Harold Keller—AGGRESSIVE BEHAVIOR:
Assessment and Intervention

C. Eugene Walker, Barbara L. Bonner & Keith L. Kaufman—
THE PHYSICALLY AND SEXUALLY ABUSED CHILD: Evaluation
and Treatment

Robert E. Becker, Richard G. Heimberg & Alan S. Bellack—SOCIAL
SKILLS TRAINING TREATMENT FOR DEPRESSION

Richard F. Dangel & Richard A. Polster—TEACHING CHILD
MANAGEMENT SKILLS

Albert Ellis, John F. McInerney, Raymond DiGiuseppe & Raymond
Yeager—RATIONAL-EMOTIVE THERAPY WITH ALCOHOLICS
AND SUBSTANCE ABUSERS

Johnny L. Matson & Thomas H. Ollendick—ENHANCING CHILDREN'S
SOCIAL SKILLS: Assessment and Training

Edward B. Blanchard, John E. Martin & Patricia M. Dubbert—NON-DRUG
TREATMENTS FOR ESSENTIAL HYPERTENSION

Samuel M. Turner & Deborah C. Beidel—TREATING OBSESSIVE-
COMPULSIVE DISORDER

Alice W. Pope, Susan M. McHale & W. Edward Craighead—SELF-
ESTEEM ENHANCEMENT WITH CHILDREN AND ADOLESCENTS

Jean E. Rhodes & Leonard A. Jason—PREVENTING SUBSTANCE
ABUSE AMONG CHILDREN AND ADOLESCENTS

Gerald D. Oster, Janice E. Caro, Daniel R. Eagen & Margaret A. Lillo—
ASSESSING ADOLESCENTS

Robin C. Winkler, Dirck W. Brown, Margaret van Keppel & Amy
Blanchard—CLINICAL PRACTICE IN ADOPTION

Roger Poppen—BEHAVIORAL RELAXATION TRAINING AND
ASSESSMENT

Michael D. LeBow—ADULT OBESITY THERAPY

Robert Paul Liberman, William J. DeRisi & Kim T. Mueser—SOCIAL
SKILLS TRAINING FOR PSYCHIATRIC PATIENTS

Johnny L. Matson—TREATING DEPRESSION IN CHILDREN AND
ADOLESCENTS

Sol L. Garfield—THE PRACTICE OF BRIEF PSYCHOTHERAPY

Arnold P. Goldstein, Barry Glick, Mary Jane Irwin,
Claudia Pask-McCartney & Ibrahim Rubama—REDUCING
DELINQUENCY: Intervention in the Community

Albert Ellis, Joyce L. Sichel, Raymond J. Yeager, Dominic J. DiMattia,
Raymond DiGiuseppe—RATIONAL-EMOTIVE COUPLES THERAPY

Clive R. Hollin—COGNITIVE-BEHAVIORAL INTERVENTIONS WITH
YOUNG OFFENDERS

Margaret P. Korb, Jeffrey Gorrell & Vernon Van De Riet—GESTALT
THERAPY: Practice and Theory, Second Edition

Donald A. Williamson—ASSESSMENT OF EATING DISORDERS
Obesity, Anorexia, and Bulimia Nervosa